LEARNING TO KNOW THE BIBLE

By
David Schroeder

FAITH AND LIFE PRESS, NEWTON, KANSAS

HERALD PRESS, SCOTTDALE, PENNSYLVANIA

Foreword

Learning to Know the Bible is the fourth of a series of six courses in the Christian Service Training Series. The first three courses have to do with *Learning to Lead, Learning to Teach,* and *Learning to Understand People.* The fifth and sixth courses will deal with *Learning to Work Together* and *Learning to Understand the Mission of the Church.*

This particular course is intended to introduce us not so much to the content of the Bible as to the many questions about the Bible that often remain untouched in our study of the Scripture. It deals with the general framework within which we need to study the Bible, and it seeks to give some of the background knowledge which will help make Bible study more meaningful.

The first three chapters begin the study by considering how God made himself known to man and how man responded to this revelation and gave witness to it. This happened long before the Scriptures in their present form were made available to man.

Chapters four to six speak to the origin of the Scriptures. Here we move from the witness that individuals gave to the revelation that they had received to the time when these accounts were collected, canonized, and recognized as sacred writings under the guidance of the Holy Spirit.

The practical use of the Bible or rather the problems related to the way the Bible speaks to us today are considered in chapters seven to nine. These chapters discuss our attitude toward Scripture, principles of interpretation, and the many disciplines that are used in the interpretation of the Scripture.

The last chapter is of a very practical nature. It seeks to introduce us to a method of Bible study which, if we make it our own and discipline ourselves to use it, will enrich our appreciation and use of the Scriptures throughout life.

I would like to give credit to my colleagues Lawrence Klippenstein and Helmut Harder for their work on chapters six and ten respectively.

Learning to Know the Bible is intended not only for teachers in the church educational program but for every person who is interested in Bible study. The book can be used as a class textbook or for individual study.

The outline for *Learning to Know the Bible* and the other courses in the Christian Service Training Series were prepared jointly by the Mennonite Board of Education and Publication, Newton, Kansas, and the Mennonite Commission for Christian Education, Scottdale, Pennsylvania. Leader's guides for these courses are also available.

D.S.

Contents

Chapter 1

God Makes Himself Known

John, the evangelist, indicates in his Gospel that "No one has ever seen God; the only Son, who is in the bosom of the Father, he has made him known" (Jn. 1:18). In other words, we know God not so much because of what we have done to search for Him, but because God chose to make himself known to us.

The Scriptures are very clear in stating that it is God who takes the initiative; it is God who reveals himself to man; it is He who comes to visit His people.

But if this is true, why is it that not more people perceive God at work in the world? Why do so many live as though there were no God? Could it be that we are often not in a position to understand the work of God because we look for answers to the wrong questions?

Notice how man-centered our questions, even our religious questions, are. We ask: "How can we know God?" "How can we find meaning in life?" "What must I do to be saved?" and "How do I know this is God's Word?" These questions are important and it is admittedly difficult to ask them in another way, for we approach everything else this way.

When we consider God's revelation of himself, however, we need to frame these questions from another perspective, a perspective that focuses on God, not man. We need to ask "How, where, and as whom has God made himself known?" We need to ask what God has done to reveal himself to man, for the Scriptures do not present God as a power, a force, or a law that has to be or can be discovered by man.

This whole self-disclosure of God to man whether in creation, history, or in Jesus Christ we call *revelation*. But the Christian church has generally distinguished between "general" and "special" revelation and it may help us to stop a few minutes with these terms.

7

General Revelation

Under the heading *general revelation* men have spoken of God's self-revelation to all men. It refers to the revelation that God has given of himself in what He has made, and in what He has done in history (Ps. 19:1; Rom. 1:18f.; Acts 14:17).

General revelation speaks of those truths that could supposedly be discovered by the unaided powers of human reason. That is, it refers to truths about God that man could perceive apart from God's revelation of himself in Christ and the Scriptures.

If there is such a revelation, however, then it should follow that everyone should be able to find God; but this does not seem to be the case. Man does not necessarily see God manifested in creation and in the events of history. Is it that God is not at work in the world anymore?

The Bible speaks to this question. From Genesis 3 on, the Bible indicates that sin has touched man's reason and understanding so that man no longer recognizes God in what He has made and in what God is even now doing in the world (Rom. 1:18ff.).

The indication is that a true knowledge of God is not possible through man's natural understanding, not because God is not acting in nature and in history, but because man in his sin and separation from God is not able to see or to perceive God. Thus, in terms of coming to know God there is no revelation of God. We must look elsewhere.

Special Revelation

His people - Isreal Church.
Events
Person - Jesus Christ.

A more meaningful term is *special revelation*. Here we speak of a special or particular revelation in which God reveals His purpose for all men in such a way that man is able to receive it and respond to it.

We said above that man in his natural state is estranged from God and, therefore, cannot see God. Before man can receive God's revelation of himself, man's sin and rebellion must be overcome and replaced by a new relationship of faith in God.

It is the essence of the gospel, good news, that, in Jesus Christ, God has dealt with sin and has opened the door to a new relationship with God. Where man accepts God's gift by faith and trust, a new understanding of God's work becomes possible.

Special revelation, therefore, says that until we accept the truth of God as it is revealed in Christ, we do not really see truth as it is. Apart from this special revelation, we view things from the perspective of our own selfishness. Special revelation is a new seeing (2 Cor. 5:17), a restoration of the powers of the mind to see higher truth; or, we might say, it is a correction of the distortions of our perverted natural vision.

Once man has received faith in God, then he also knows Him to be the Creator. Then man recognizes that "the heavens are telling the glory of God; and the firmament proclaims his handiwork" (Ps. 19:1).

In the same way, the eye of faith can recognize God's revelation of himself in the events of history. Without this faith the same events are simply ascribed to natural laws, fate, or pure chance. It was the understanding of faith that permitted Israel to see God at work in the call of Abraham (Gen. 12); the deliverance (Exodus), and the covenant. Even the times of judgment and captivity were seen to be God's hand punishing Israel for their unfaithfulness in the keeping of the covenant they had made with God. It is through self-revelation that we know God and can relate to Him.

How Has God Revealed Himself?

We return now to the specific question of how God has revealed himself. The answer is that He has revealed himself as some *one,* as personal being, as the living God.

Knowledge of God is not to be received in the way that we gain a knowledge of things. We do not know God in the way that we know the world. God is not "manifest" in the same way as physical objects are manifest. Knowledge of God is more

9

than factual knowledge; it is like knowledge received in and about personal relationships.

Living persons cannot be known in terms of abstractions. We can say, for instance, that someone else is loving, kind, and trustworthy, but these terms do not take on real meaning until they become known in concrete actions of that person.

In the same way God did not first of all reveal himself to man in terms of general statements describing His attributes. God made himself known to man in what He did for His people. He became known to the Israelites as He acted decisively in their struggle for survival, first in Egypt, then in the wilderness, and finally in the promised land. That God was redeemer and Lord became clear to them in their experience of liberation and redemption.

It is because God is the living Lord that no attempt is made in Scripture to give a definition of what God is or proof that He exists. If God is to be known, His story must be told, that is, we must look at the events in the life of the people and nation with which God has been in conversation. Because God makes himself known in specific acts and particular events, His presence, His character, and His unique reality can only be disclosed by narrating the events which bear witness to Him.

The writer to the Hebrews indicates that God revealed himself "in many and various ways" (Heb. 1:1). God is not bound in the way in which He makes himself known. He comes to one person in a dream (Joseph), a deep sleep (Job), in a burning bush (Moses) or in a spoken word of the prophet. Finally, He came in the flesh, but always this revelation is given in a concrete situation in history.

Not every vision or dream, however, is a revelation of God. The form does not guarantee the event. Yet any event can become the medium of God's revelation when God chooses to make it such and when man becomes aware of God's action and responds to it in faith and trust.

We have said that God makes himself known in particular events in history. If this is correct, we should be able to say where He has revealed himself. It is the affirmation of the Scriptures that God has made himself known in His relations with the children of Israel.

God's revelation of himself does not come to men in general, but it comes in specific events, to specific persons. To make himself known, God chose some particular place and some particular relationship. The Scriptures indicate that God made himself known to one person—to Abraham and through him to the people of Israel.

We do not know why God chose Israel and not another nation. It was not because of any great merit on Israel's part as they well knew (Deut. 7:7). We do not even know whether God tried to make himself known to others in the same way. We only know that He chose Israel as the people to whom and through whom He made himself known.

Israel, nevertheless, did supply one element that was essential in God's revelation of himself. There could be no revelation of God apart from those who responded in faith and trust to God's manifestation of himself.

Events alone do not make a revelation. Man must discern God in and beyond the events in which He becomes manifest. God revealing and man receiving and responding must be simultaneously present for a revelation to occur.

Thus, if we are to know God, we will need to depend on the testimony of those who have come to know God in a particular experience or event in history. Beginning with Abraham, we will be able to see God revealing himself to man, as man is able to perceive Him and to respond to Him in faith and obedience. We will be able to see also that man receives a growing knowledge of God over the centuries until finally the time is ripe when God can reveal himself in the flesh and when some would be prepared to receive Him as the Son of God and not as an imposter.

As Whom Has God Revealed Himself?

God has shown himself to Israel as the living Lord of history; He is Sovereign Lord of all; He is the creator and sustainer but also the redeemer and Saviour of His people.

This question will be considered at greater length in the next two chapters. We need to follow the history of God's revelation to Israel and finally to all men in Christ. It is as we look at this history of revelation (Heilsgeschichte) that we will be able to see more clearly as whom God has revealed himself.

Revelation and the Bible

From what we have said thus far, it is evident that the revelation of God preceded the Bible. There was first of all the manifestation of God in the events of history and man's response of faith to that revelation before the revelation could be communicated to others. Jacob met God at Bethel, and the children of Israel met God in the exodus long before there were any written accounts of these events that could be read by others.

After the initial revelatory event, there was often a period of time when the testimony of what God had done was passed on by word of mouth from one generation to the next before it was finally put into the written form we have today. We must not forget that there were hundreds of years between Abraham and Moses, and between Moses and the latter prophets or historians.

This poses a question for us as to how we shall view the Bible. How is it related to revelation? Is it possible to separate the two—to take one and leave the other?

The tendency has been for us to see revelation entirely as God communicating eternal truths about himself through the writers of Scripture. In this sense revelation is seen as occurring primarily at the point of writing. But if we say revelation occurred in the writing only, then the Scriptures would be speaking about God largely in abstractions. The words that the writers use to describe the nature of God would have to be filled with meaning from our own everyday experience. (See page 10 above.)

12

If God spoke first in words or writings, then it would be sufficient to regard the events recorded in Scripture as mere illustrations of what was meant by the words. The events would then not need to be historical events at all to fulfill their purpose. The actual situation, however, is the reverse of this. God acted in history and man recognized God's revelation of himself, responded to it in faith, and spoke about it. It is in this way that we come to have the Scriptures in their present form.

Revelation must be seen, therefore, as God's activity in human life that reached its highest point when God himself became flesh in Jesus Christ. The Bible is the message of what God has done for man but is also itself one of the acts of God in giving to man a revelation of himself and in redeeming man.

Because revelation is prior to the Scripture, there is the opposite danger of seeing revelation as given only in the events, only in the experience of encounter with God. In so viewing revelation, Scripture becomes merely a record of the revelation. It is true, Scripture is a record of this revelation, but it is not merely that. It is much more than an account of someone's impressions of what happened.

We could say rather "the Bible is the message about this action; but this message is itself an action of God."[1] The event of revelation, which includes act and word, cannot be separated from the understanding of the event and from its interpretation. The event in a sense controls the meaning of the word, or fills it with meaning; whereas the words about events help us to understand the events themselves. Event and interpretation of the event, therefore, cannot be separated, or both lose their significance.

Revelation is the more inclusive term covering the whole distance from the event of revelation to its authentic record in Scripture. In this sense the Bible participates also in the revelation itself and is in addition the medium through which the knowledge of this revelation is communicated to all men.

The Scriptures do not leave us in any doubt as to the authority of the Bible. Early in their history the people of God covenanted to keep the Law of Moses (Ex. 24:7). Later they accepted in the same way the rest of the Old and New Testament.

In the New Testament the authority of Jesus is everywhere lifted up. Jesus himself says, "All authority in heaven and on earth has been given to me" (Mt. 28:18). Even the Pharisees recognize that He taught as one having authority.

We notice further that Jesus delegated authority to the apostles as He sent them out in His name (Lk. 10:17), and many signs and wonders were performed by them (Acts 5:12). Paul even says: "The signs of a true apostle were performed among you in all patience, with signs and wonders and mighty works" (2 Cor. 12:12). This same authority is also claimed for the apostolic writings, for Paul writes: "So then, brethren, stand firm and hold to the traditions which you were taught by us, either by word of mouth or by letter" (2 Thess. 2:15).

If the Scriptures are authoritative and binding on the church, are they also binding on all people? To this we must answer both "yes" and "no." Yes, it is authoritative to the one who has accepted Jesus Christ as Lord and Saviour. The answer is "no" for those who do not receive Jesus Christ or the Scriptures as a word from God.

The statements about the authority of the Scriptures, as found in the Bible, are meaningful to those who accept the Bible as God's Word, but not to those who do not already accept its authority. We must, therefore, speak to the question of authority in another way, for the authority of the Scriptures is related to the question of faith in Christ.

The writer of the Book of Hebrews speaks to this question in Hebrews 2:1-4. He indicates first of all that the message recorded in the New Testament had its beginning with Jesus Christ (2:3b). He is undoubtedly referring to the teachings of Jesus. Secondly, he states that this gospel was faithfully transmitted to the writers by those who heard Him. Those who wrote the books of the New Testament have received an accurate account of the events that transpired. But more must be said.

The third statement he makes is the more significant for us in speaking about the authority of Scripture. He says, "God also bore witness by signs and wonders and various miracles and by the gifts of the Holy Spirit distributed according to his own will" (Heb. 2:4). This indicates that it is God who works in us the miracle of faith; it is God who works in us the miracle of accepting the Scriptures as God's Word. It is only after we have received this testimony of the Holy Spirit in our spirit that we truly accept God's Word as authoritative and binding upon our lives. Once we have accepted Christ, and this miracle of faith has been performed in us, then all the references to the authority of God's Word become meaningful to us.

We see operative here what has been called the self-authenticating nature of Scriptures. It is not man's arguments, nor the number of quotations that he can cite, that convince men of the authority of God's Word; it is rather the revelation of God in our own hearts, to which we respond in faith, that makes us accept the Bible as God's Word and that makes us yield our lives in obedience to that Word under the guidance of the Spirit of Christ.

For Further Study

Barth, Karl. *God in Action*. Des Moines: (Channel) Meredith, 1963. See specifically the chapter on Revelation, p. 3.

Bender, Harold S. *Biblical Revelation and Inspiration*. Scottdale: Herald Press, Focal Pamphlet No. 4, 1959.

Foreman, Kenneth J. "What Is the Bible?" in *Introduction to the Bible*. Vol. 1 of the *Layman's Bible Commentary*, edited by Balmer H. Kelly. Richmond: John Knox Press, 1959.*

Geldenhuys, J. Norval. *Supreme Authority*. Grand Rapids: Eerdmans, 1953.

Henry, Carl F. H., ed. *Revelation and the Bible*. Grand Rapids: Baker Book House, 1958.

Johnson, Douglas. *The Christian and His Bible.* Grand Rapids: Eerdmans, 1953.

Nygren, Anders. *The Significance of the Bible for the Church.* Philadelphia: Fortress Press, 1963.*

Wenger, J. C. *God's Word Written.* Scottdale: Herald Press, 1966.*

---

*Recommended for the church library.

1 Anders Nygren, *The Significance of the Bible for the Church* (Philadelphia, Fortress Press, 1963), p. 7.

Chapter 2

God Chooses a People

God made himself known to the people of Israel. He did so in events that could be seen by all. It is, therefore, possible to give an account of this revelation in the long history of the people of Israel. Because of this fact, it is not surprising that much of the Bible is written as historical narrative: it is telling this story.

The Bible tells us about events that really happened, and about people who were very much a part of their world. It is a selective history, however, for not all events nor all the people involved are mentioned. The writers appear to have selected certain events and experiences which became unusually meaningful and significant as carriers of the Word of God to man. In certain events the acts of God became transparent or visible and they testify to God's dealings with man. It will be helpful, therefore, to review this history of special events to which Israel referred in speaking of God's revelation.

The Setting

The story of God's revelation touches specific times and places. Geographically, the account begins in the so-called Ancient Near East or the present-day Middle East. It includes the area known today as Iraq, Iran, Turkey, Jordan, Israel, Saudi Arabia, and Egypt. The whole Old Testament history takes place in a rough rectangle of land five hundred miles from north to south and one thousand miles from east to west.

This part of the world had three foci: Egypt, Syria-Palestine, and Mesopotamia. Restricted by the desert and the sea, trade movements and life in general moved along a narrow fertile crescent. Beginning with the Nile Valley the fertile crescent stretches north and eastward to include the Sinai Peninsula and the coastal region of Syria-Palestine, and then curves back southeastward along the valley of the two rivers: the Tigris and Euphrates. (It would help to consult a map at this point).

Several adjoining regions might be mentioned also. One is the great sandy plateau, the Arabian Desert, the original home of the Semitic nomads who settled and developed the Mesopotamian valley. Then there are the plains and the hill country of Syria-Palestine. The region later known as Asia Minor, though of lesser significance in Old Testament times, plays a prominent role in the New Testament.

The Old Testament focuses on the "bridge" between the two great civilization centers of Egypt and Mesopotamia. Known first as Canaan and then as Palestine, this land is only 150 miles long and varies from 25 to 50 miles in width, a small country indeed. To the west lies the Mediterranean Sea, to the east the vast Transjordan desert. It stretches from Lake Huleh in the north down to the Gulf of Aqabah and the Red Sea in the south. A line of hills runs the full length of the land along the Jordan valley. The coastal region is broken up into the Plain of Acco, the Plain of Sharon, and the Plain of Philistia.

This was the home of the Hebrews and their "promised land."

The Call of the Fathers

The Hebrews traced their history back to the period of their "fathers," Abraham, Isaac, and Jacob (Deut. 26:5), whose ancestors came from Ur in southern Mesopotamia (Gen. 11:31). God's revelation of himself to a people begins with His command to Abraham to leave kin and country and to journey to a land that God would give him (Gen. 12:1ff.).

It is evident immediately that in the call of Abraham God is dealing with the whole world. He starts with one man, one family, one nation; but His concern is that all the families of the earth shall be blessed (Gen. 12:3). As sin entered by the disobedience of one (Adam), so righteousness would be won by the obedience of one (Jesus) who would come from this people that God had called to himself.

The Pentateuch, the first five books of the Bible, shows the faith of the fathers as they responded in obedience to God's call. But the central person in the entire account is God himself. He shows himself to be the God who calls them to a new land, who provides for their needs and shows himself faithful in fulfilling His promise to Abraham, Isaac, and Jacob.

Why God Called a People

The first eleven chapters of Genesis are a prologue to this history of revelation. They indicate why it was necessary for God to begin again with one man, Abraham, in His dealings with man. This introduction to the Bible has much to say to us.

The prologue tells us who God is:

1. God is the creator. He created the heavens and the earth. Even the sun, moon, and stars which others worshiped as gods were created by God (Gen. 1:1, 14, 16).

2. God is sovereign Lord. He rules over all that He has made. He is the sustainer of life.

3. God is a God of order. He ordered everything. All chaos was dispelled: sea and earth were separated, as was light from darkness. All living things were made to reproduce after their own kind (Gen. 1).

4. God created everything "good" (Gen. 1:31). It was good and even now God seeks the well-being of His creatures. He gives to all life and breath and food to eat (Gen. 1:30, 2:9a). God blesses what He had made (Gen. 1:22, 28; 2:3).

The Prologue tells us what man is:

1. Man is made in the image of God. He is made to have dominion over the rest of creation as a servant of God (Gen. 1:26-31).

2. Man is a personal being who may have communion with God, though he, too, is a creature made out of the dust of the earth. He has freedom to respond to God but his welfare is

19

dependent on his obedience to God. To disobey is to invite death (Gen. 2:16, 17).

3. Man is estranged from God. Through disobedience man disrupted his fellowship with God. He has sinned and hides himself from God (Gen. 3:1-13). This sin eats into all man's relationships: man and wife (Adam-Eve), brother and brother (Cain-Abel), and man and his fellowmen (Noah-Nephilim).

The Prologue tells us that God seeks to save man:

1. Genesis 5-11 tells us that God is a judge of all sin (Cain's banishment, the flood, the tower of Babel), but also a gracious Saviour. The evil serpent is destined to be defeated (Gen. 3:15). Noah and his family are saved and God gives man another opportunity (Gen. 9:1, 8-17). God is not a destroyer of life; on the contrary, He wishes to redeem man (Gen. 8:21).

2. Not all the questions that we might ask about the origin of evil are answered in the prologue. It does, however, explain God's purposes and His dealings with man. It shows man's distorted knowledge of God and the need for a new revelation (Gen. 11:1-9).

Thus it is with great expectation that we look to God for a new beginning after we have seen how man has become bankrupt in his own self-reliance. God begins again with one man of faith, with one man who hears and obeys His voice, with one man who trusts in God. It is through Abraham's response of faith that God chose for himself a people to whom and through whom He would reveal himself.

The question of how Genesis 1 relates to our questions about science will be discussed briefly in chapter 9.

Israel Becomes a Covenant People

The patriarchal period lasted for two centuries or longer. In a time of great famine, Jacob and his sons left Palestine for Egypt. Here Joseph, the second youngest son, became a mighty ruler in the land. The time was *ca.* 1700 B.C.

Historians link this time with the invasion of Egypt by the Hyksos under whom Joseph found favor. Later, however, the

Egyptians under Seti I and Ramses II (*ca.* 1290-1224 B.C.) tried with much fighting to regain their land. The Hebrews were regarded as foreign enemies and subjected to slavery. They were used in building defense works and cities such as Pithom and Raamses (Ex. 1:11).

It was in this situation that they cried to God for help. God heard their cry and called Moses to lead this people out of Egypt. Moses was a Hebrew who had been adopted by the royal family. In a unique personal encounter (Ex. 3:1-15), God introduced himself to Moses as "I AM WHO I AM" and stated His plan for Israel. God promised to save His people and to be with Moses with signs and wonders.

Moses, in the name of God, dared to challenge Pharaoh to let the people go. Pharaoh resisted; but the hand of God, through plagues and the powers of nature, was not to be denied. Moses led the people through the parted waters of the Red Sea waterway. Their pursuers were halted and prevented from following. God had set His people free. They sang the song of victory (Ex. 15). Forevermore Israel would look on this event as the clearest evidence that God was their Saviour, Redeemer, and Lord. So they sang: "The Lord is my strength and my song, and he has become my salvation" (Ex. 15:2).

When they reached Mount Sinai, a high mountain region where Moses had first heard his call, God spoke to Israel through Moses on the basis of what He had already done for them.

"Thus you shall say to the house of Jacob, and tell the people of Israel: You have seen what I did to the Egyptians, and how I bore you on eagles' wings and brought you to myself. Now therefore, if you will obey my voice and keep my covenant, you shall be my own possession among all peoples; for all the earth is mine, and you shall be to me a kingdom of priests and a holy nation" (Ex. 19:3-6).

God gave Moses the law, which told Israel how they were to govern their lives in this kingdom of God's rule. Moses read the commands of God to the people who covenanted to keep all that God had commanded (Ex. 19:8; 24:3). Thus, Israel had not only become a new nation but a nation which covenanted to be God's own people.

The idea of covenant was familiar in those days. A victorious nation would often set up stipulations under which they would be gracious to a captured nation. Similarly God had chosen for himself a people and His relations to the people would be governed by His covenant. The proper response to what God had done was at first summarily expressed in the Ten Commandments and then enlarged to cover all of the civil and religious life of the people. Israel had become a theocracy, a nation under God. It was a covenant made in fulfillment of the covenant with Abraham (Ex. 2:24).

Israel saw that they were not only a people delivered out of bondage but a people who had been redeemed for a purpose. They had received a mission: to be a mirror of God's goodness and mercy, to be the people through whom the promise to Abraham should be fulfilled. In the covenant God had pledged His perpetual blessing and support. As long as Israel would respond in obedient faith God's blessing was assured.

Israel Inherits the Land

After a sojourn of forty years in the wilderness, the Israelites entered Canaan. The Books of Joshua and Judges record this invasion. The Mer-ne-Ptah Stele (Israel Stele) shows that they were in the land in the fifth year of Mer-ne-Ptah or 1220 B.C. The conquest began with the defeat of the kings of the Transjordan, Sihon and Og (Deut. 2:26-3:11). Crossing the Jordan, Joshua took Jericho and with it central Palestine. A thrust south and then north established them in the land (Josh. 1-12), even though pockets of territory remained to be taken (Judg. 1:8-21), and they had to live with other people.

The land was divided among the tribes, and a nomadic people sought to became an agricultural people. In so doing they were again and again tempted to worship the gods of the people who had lived in the land. Were theirs not the gods who provided the fertility of the land? This was an easy step to take because the Israelites were trying hard in every way to reach the level of culture that the other peoples had already attained.

During this time Palestine was often harassed, raided, and plundered by neighboring hostile people such as the Midianites, Ammonites, and Philistines. It was in this time of storm and stress that the judges gave leadership to the twelve tribes. God sent them leaders such as Gideon, Deborah, and Samson whenever the people turned from their sin and cried to God for deliverance.

Again, all such conquests were seen as the fulfillment of the promise to Abraham: "To your descendants I will give this land" (Gen. 12:7). As long as the people kept the covenant they were strong in the Lord. But when they denied God and quarreled with each other they became weak and were preyed upon by their enemies. God revealed to them that disobedience and unbelief carry their own punishment.

A Nation Under Kings

The twelve tribes were at first united not only by a common ancestry, but even more by their common relationship to God in the covenant. But as they lived in the land the bonds which united them tended to disappear. Finally, Samuel, one of the greatest leaders since Moses, was about the only one who still worked with all the tribes.

The cry for a new nationalism became louder. The people were calling for a king. Samuel saw this as taking a step away from God, but finally became himself the bridge between the period of the judges and the kings. He insisted that any king who would reign must see himself as under the covenant which God made with Israel.

Saul, the first king, though successful in restraining the Philistines, was rejected because he did not carry out the ban against enriching themselves on the spoils of other peoples. In this sense he foreshadowed the monarchy in Israel. There are, however, a few bright spots in the history of the nation. Standing out above all is King David who brought Israel to the peak of its imperial glory. David not only extended the Empire in every direction, but he took Jerusalem and established it as the Holy City. In his obedience to God he foreshadowed what God had in mind for the Messiah to accomplish; in his disobedience he foreshadowed the way in which God would deal with the sinner who confesses to God.

Solomon took over from a model ruler. He launched a vast program of government construction, political consolidation, trade and commerce, mining, and the building of the temple. His policies resulted in heavy taxation, forced labor, public resentment; and, gradually, segments of the kingdom were lost. During his time, however, the temple and its ritual were established.

When Solomon died in 922 B.C., the kingdom split into two parts. The northern ten tribes seceded and chose Jeroboam I as king. Rehoboam, Solomon's son, retained the two tribes, Benjamin and Judah, in the south.

The historians of Israel agreed that none of the kings of the Northern Kingdom did what was right before God. Assyria became a dominant power at this time.

Omri and Ahab, together with their neighbors held back Assyria for a while and Jehu and Jeroboam II were able to extend its borders and make it a prosperous nation, in spite of the threat of Assyrian domination. Nevertheless, the nation, because of its social, political, and religious practices, had become internally weak and could not long maintain itself.

Into this situation the prophet came with a word from God. Elijah spoke to Ahab and warned him against worshiping false gods (1 Kings 18:21ff.). Amos also listed the sins of the Northern Kingdom and pronounced God's judgment (Amos 2:6ff.). A nation that has deserted the covenant cannot enjoy God's divine protection. In 722 B.C. Samaria, its capital, fell to the Assyrians. The inhabitants were taken away never to return, and others were brought in to take their place.

The prophets were intent on calling Israel and Judah back to keeping the covenant and to warn them of what would happen

24

if they would disregard it. Where there was no regard for justice and righteousness, whether in royal court or humble cottage, there the wrath of God would be visited upon the people. The prophets interpreted to Israel the meaning of the covenant with respect to their own history. It was a new word from God. They spoke with authority their "Thus saith the Lord."

Into Exile and the Return

Judah, the Southern Kingdom, escaped the fate of the Northern Kingdom for over a century. In 612 B.C. the Babylonians took over the eastern kingdoms. Palestine, too, found itself under Babylonian domination, a situation which was not looked on with kindness by the ultrapatriots of Judah. Jeremiah spoke in favor of loyalty to Babylon, but his word was not heeded.

Rebellions against Babylon on the part of Jehoiakim and Zedekiah caused the city to be taken and burned and its people taken into exile to Babylon. This happened in spite of the efforts of Jeremiah, Obadiah, and other prophets seeking to call Israel to a new obedience to God.

Babylon became the new "home" for thousands of Judean exiles for the next fifty years. By 539 B.C. a new power, the Persian, set up one of the greatest empires the world had known. It was not to be dissolved till 333 B.C. in the time of Alexander the Great.

In Babylon the voice of the prophet continued to be heard. With the help of the Prophets such as Ezekiel and Deutero-Isaiah, Israel reflected on what had happened in Canaan. As a result, they turned back to the fundamentals of the faith. They even organized the synagogue in Babylon to speak actively to the propagation of the faith.

When the Persians took over power from the Babylonians, the Israelites were permitted to return to Jerusalem. Nehemiah and Ezra worked hard to restore first the temple and the city walls and even harder to establish the Law as the central, controlling factor in the life of the people.

Now the people saw once more the hand of God. They accepted the prophetic message that the exile had been God's judgment for allowing the covenant to be neglected in their daily activities and political action. But now in the valley of dry bones there was new life. God had not really deserted His people. The remnant was not lost. In His grace God had purified His people and called them into a closer relationship to Him.

Through a long course of political and national events, God had carefully carried forward His plans. History was still in His hands and Israel had received more and more of God's revelation of himself. They could see that God had been with them, had been in their midst, had participated in their very life. He had sought to prosper His people spiritually and materially and to lead them to the fulfillment of the mission to which He had called them. Unbelief and disobedience often brought sorrow and ruin to the people, but they began to see also that faithfulness to the covenant relationship brought glory and blessing.

The destiny of this people, they began to understand, lay in the hands of their God. In their history and experience they had seen His hand. Man might accept Him or reject Him, but God alone could save.

For Further Study

Anderson, B. W. *Understanding the Old Testament.* Englewood Cliffs: Prentice-Hall, 1957.

Bruce, F. F. *Israel and the Nations.* Grand Rapids: Eerdmans, 1963.*

Foreman, Kenneth J., et al. *Introduction to the Bible.* Vol. 1 of *Layman's Bible Commentary.* Richmond: John Knox Press, 1959.

Rhodes, Arnold. *The Mighty Acts of God.* Richmond: John Knox Press, 1964.

Richardson, Alan. *A Preface to the Bible.* Philadelphia: Westminster Press, 1944.

Rowley, Harold H. *The Faith of Israel.* London: Student Christian Movement, 1956.*

Rowley, Harold H. *The Unity of the Bible.* New York: Meridian, 1957.

Westermann, Claus. *A Thousand Years and a Day.* Philadelphia: Fortress, 1962.

Wright, G. E. and Filson, F. V., eds. *Westminster Historical Maps of Bible Lands.* Philadelphia: Westminster, 1952.*

---

*Recommended for the church library.

Chapter 3

The Supreme Revelation

The Christian church has always seen the fulfillment of God's revelation as occurring in Jesus Christ the Son of God. This revelation is recorded in the New Testament. In Christ the whole action of God in history receives its basic purpose. The years of preparation had been long. "But when the time had fully come, God sent forth his Son" (Gal. 4:4). This new revelation in Christ was recognized and acknowledged by the writer of Hebrews: "In many and various ways God spoke of old to our fathers by the prophets; but in these last days he has spoken to us by a Son" (Heb. 1:1, 2).

Between the Testaments

When the last of the Old Testament books was written, it was as if prophecy ceased until John the Baptist came in the same tradition. But we should not think that things had come to a standstill. Life continued and further political, social, and religious developments set the stage for much that we find in the New Testament.

The chief source of information for this period is I Maccabees, one of the books of the Apocrypha. It tells us of the conquests of Alexander the Great and of the division of the realm among his successors in the three kingdoms of Macedonia, Syria, and Egypt (1:1-9). It tells further of the Maccabean revolt under Judas Maccabeus and his brothers Jonathan and Simon. It was at this time when Israel for a few short years (143-63 B.C.) was again an independent nation as in the days of King David.

During this time Judaism took on the forms which are visible in New Testament times. Though the temple was still symbolically the center of religious life, the real center must now be seen in the synagogue which had been developed during the Exile. It served well in a time of dispersion. The synagogues were run by elders (*presbyteros,* from which we get the words *priest* and *presbyter*) who had power to excommunicate.

The Great Sanhedrin was the official ruling body of Jewry and we meet the activities of this group in "the chief priests and elders and scribes" of the Gospels. Depending on the political rulers in power, this group had or did not have the right to carry out the death penalty. It was in the intertestamental period that the diverse religio-political views of the major sects in Judaism (Pharisees, Scribes, Sadducees, Zealots, Essenes) emerged and crystallized.

Religiously, the intertestamental period represented a life-and-death struggle against Hellenistic (Greek) secularism and religious syncretism (the fusing of different religions). The Pharisees sought to speak to it by applying to new situations ancient Jewish laws, which had been intended for a more primitive society. They would repeat the interpretation of the law given earlier and then add new ones of their own to cover new contingencies. All of this led to legalism and to a belief in the saving value of good works.

Another form of literature, called apocalyptic literature, was written during the intertestamental period. It began already in the Old Testament with the Book of Daniel. Here the teachings are couched in the form of visions granted to great men of the past (Enoch, Moses, Ezra, etc.). This device was chosen because they held that the period of revelation had closed with the law and the prophets. It was thus written in the name and spirit of someone recognized in the canon. This literature looks to the day when God in a sudden and violent way will usher in His kingdom.

The Birth of Jesus

That the promise given to Abraham and the fulfillment of prophecy should come in the birth of a child in Bethlehem just before 4 B.C. was unexpected to say the least. Yet in this time when Caesar Augustus ruled the Empire and just before the death of King Herod who ruled under him in Judea, Joseph and Mary made their historic journey from Nazareth, their home, to Bethlehem.

The Gospels center mainly on the works and words of Jesus and on His passion, death, and resurrection. In fact Mark and John tell us nothing at all about the details of Jesus' birth. Even Matthew and Luke tell us very little when we consider the length of time Israel had waited for their Messiah. In the Gospels there is no preoccupation with his parents, his early years, or his training. His mission to the world is what is important.

It appears as if many of the items mentioned in the account of His birth were made necessary by the opposition to and rejection of the gospel. Thus, the writers show that Jesus was of the proper lineage (Mt. 1:1-17; Lk. 3:23-38); that He was not an illegitimate son but was conceived by the Holy Spirit (Mt. 1:18ff.); that there were attestations to His divinity already at the time of His birth (the testimony of the shepherds, the Magi, Simeon, Anna, Elizabeth, and Mary herself); that He was brought up as a son of the law (He was taken to study the law at age of twelve.); and above all, angelic visitors had both announced and attended His coming (Lk. 1:26ff.; 2:13ff.) and even gave His name as Jesus "for he will save his people from their sins" (Mt. 1:21).

His Public Ministry

The way for the revelation to come in Christ was prepared by John the Baptist (*ca.* A.D. 27) when Jesus was "about thirty years of age" (Lk. 3:23). This was the beginning of the fulfillment of the prophetic word (Mal. 3:1; Isa. 40:3). John called the people to repent and to be baptized, confessing their sins. It represented a break with Judaism as then practiced. It was a call to again cross the Jordan into a new land. Many heeded this call of John.

30

In His baptism Jesus identifies with this new movement. In His baptism, as later in His death, he was identified with "transgressors." The baptism marks the anointing for service and the beginning of Jesus' ministry. A voice from heaven clearly indicates that Jesus is the Messiah, the suffering servant of God, by the statement, "Thou art my beloved Son; with thee I am well pleased" (Mk. 1:9-11). This statement combines Psalm 2, which was used in the anointing of a king, and the ordination formula of Isaiah 42:1.

But Satan is not willing to have even one person do the will of God. It is thus not strange to see the temptation scene follow immediately upon baptism (Mk. 1:12, 13). Jesus' victory here foreshadows both the passion of our Lord and His victory over sin and death. Mark shows clearly that from here on, the evil spirits recognize Jesus as the Son of God (Mk. 1:12, 13, 23-25, 34; 3:11, 12; 5:6-8). Yet He tells them to be silent and not to speak of His true identity.

For man to recognize that Jesus was the Christ took much longer. To lead man to see in Him the Son of God was the purpose of Jesus' earthly ministry. Jesus, therefore, comes with the message "repent and believe in the gospel." Yet Jesus was not only calling men to believe "something," He was calling them to himself so that one day they would see in Him the Messiah.

To reveal himself to man Jesus did all the works of the Messiah. He healed the sick (Mk. 1:29-31, 32-34, 40-45; 2:1-12; 3:1-5; 5:25-34); He cast out demons (Mk. 1:23-28, 32-34; 3:11, 22-30; 5:2-20; 7:25-30); and raised the dead (Mk. 5:22-24; 35-43).

Yet the results are not an immediate recognition of His messiahship. It is reported by Mark that the people are astonished at His power and authority, but that they do not know who He is (Mk. 1:27; 2:12; 5:20, 42; 6:14-16; 7:37). His fame spreads afar but not a true knowledge of Him (Mk. 1:28, 37, 45; 3:7; 5:20; 6:14-16, 54-56; 7:24-37). Even the disciples do not recognize Him for what He is (Mk. 4:41; 6:51, 52; 8:17-21).

Similarly Jesus teaches His disciples and indicates that He has power to forgive sins (Mk. 2:1-12); that He is the bridegroom and brings in a new era (new wine, Mk. 2:18-22); and that He is the one who brings healing to the sinner (Mk. 2:17f.). But they do not yet link all of this with the fact that He is the Messiah. Eventually, however, His words and His works compel men to make a decision. They have really only two options: either He does His works in the power of Satan or in the power of God. There were those who said that "He is possessed by Beelzebul, and by the prince of demons he casts out the demons" (Mk. 3:22). Others decided He was only an ordinary man, in fact, the carpenter's son (Mk. 6:1-6). Jesus seems to be more readily accepted beyond the borders of Israel than by His own people (Mk. 7:24-30). After all the signs of the Messiah that Jesus had already given, the Pharisees still come and ask for a sign from heaven (Mk. 8:11-13).

After several years of teaching and observing the works of the Messiah, the Spirit of God had worked in the disciples the miracle of faith. They had come to see in Jesus the Messiah of God. When Jesus asks "But who do you say that I am?", Peter replies "You are the Christ" (Mk. 8:29).

The life of Jesus did not automatically convince men of His divinity no more than the events of history in the life of Israel convinced everyone that God was with them. Such vision was born of faith. To be able to see the physical events as the vehicle of revelation was the gift of the Spirit. Thus Jesus indicates to Peter "flesh and blood has not revealed this to you" (Mt. 16:17).

The moment the disciples received in Jesus the revelation of God, the earthly ministry of Jesus had accomplished its intended purpose. From here on Jesus indicated that He must suffer and die (Mk. 8:31; 9:31; 10:33) and be raised again on the third day.

Jesus' Passion and Death

For the disciples Good Friday and Easter were as unexpected as they were hard to explain. Peter could not accept the an-

32

nouncement of Jesus that He must suffer. "Far be it from thee," he answers Jesus. Peter did not understand that "God so loved the world that he gave his only Son" (Jn. 3:16); he did not understand that love and obedience to God's will of necessity took Jesus to the cross.

Jesus came to reveal the love of God. He revealed to man a new self-sacrificing love. He came to win man with love. The depth of God's love is seen in Jesus' love even for those who rejected Him and said "no" to His message. For those who crucified Him, He prayed "Father, forgive them; for they know not what they do" (Lk. 23:34).

Man's love is not like this. When our will is thwarted and our good intentions rejected, we are ready with the disciples to call down fire from heaven. Man's love so easily turns to hate, or fear, and resorts to force and compulsion to gain its way. Not so, the love of God.

Peter indicates how the love of Jesus did not change even while He was reviled, beaten, and slain (1 Pet. 2:21-25). Paul emphasized that through this obedience, an obedience unto death, a new righteousness was made possible (Rom. 5:19; cf. Heb. 10:1-10).

The Gospels make it abundantly clear that Jesus could have chosen another way. In His temptation He was offered the kingdoms of the world if He would fall down and worship Satan; at the feeding of the five thousand they desired to make Him king; at the time when Jesus was taken captive He indicates that He could call down legions of angels, but He purposely chose not to go another way. In the garden He prayed and chose to do the will of the Father.

Jesus suffered the worst that sin could do. He suffered death as an innocent man at the hands of men who hated Him. In so doing, He revealed a new love to mankind. It was a self-giving, worth-bestowing, sacrificial love. Some of this is recognized even by the centurion at the cross when he said "Truly this was the Son of God!" (Mt. 27:54).

Later the disciples realized that Jesus had, in going the way of the cross, fulfilled the promise and prophecy of the Old Covenant. This did not become clear to them, however, until after the resurrection. This revelation was yet to come.

The Resurrection

Long before His crucifixion, Jesus had indicated that He would rise again from the dead. All such comments, however, held little meaning for the disciples. Even after His death and burial they talked as though they had been mistaken about Jesus. "But we had hoped that he was the one to redeem Israel" (Lk. 24:21).

The appearances of the resurrected Lord to Mary (Mk. 16:1ff.), to the Emmaus disciples, and to the eleven disciples (Lk. 24:28-43) convinced them of the mighty act of God in raising Jesus from the dead. They recognized His voice, they recognized Him in the breaking of the bread, and they could no longer deny that "The Lord has risen indeed."

Few of the events in the life of Christ are as well attested to as His resurrection appearances. This was the cornerstone of all that God had done and would be the first to be denied by unbelief. Yet even Thomas, who did not at first accept the message, responds with the testimony "my Lord and my God" when Jesus appears to him.

The disciples and those with them had seen the risen Lord. Much of what they had been taught now fell into place. But Jesus remained with them forty days in which "he opened their minds to understand the scriptures" (Lk. 24:44-47).

Now they began to see how the birth, life and ministry, death and resurrection of Christ had both been promised and foretold. Now they saw how the sacrifice in Israel was a foreshadowing of the once-for-all sacrifice of Christ. They understood further the commission to be witnesses unto all people. With the teaching of Jesus after the resurrection a process had begun in the disciples in which the Spirit of God would continue to lead them: the process of seeing how Scripture had been and was being fulfilled.

Pentecost and Proclamation

Pentecost fulfilled the prophecy of Joel, that the Spirit of God would come upon His people. In this a new people was born. In this the church was born and also received its anointing to preach the gospel to all people.

In the Book of Acts we see first of all the account of how the Spirit of God came upon the waiting disciples and empowered them to speak by the power of the Holy Spirit. Hearts were touched again and again with the gospel message and daily "the Lord added to their number . . . those who were being saved" (Acts 2:47).

This witness is next taken across the gulf that separated Jew and Gentile. The Holy Spirit comes upon Cornelius, a Gentile, through the ministry of Peter (Acts 10). Such action is later verified in greater depth in the Jerusalem Council (Acts 15). All have become one in Christ.

Missionaries are finally sent out to proclaim the gospel in all the then known world. They sound out the message that Christ has died for all and that "God was in Christ reconciling the world to himself" (2 Cor. 5:19). They understood very clearly that they had been called to be ambassadors for Christ, beseeching men to turn to Christ (2 Cor. 5:18-20).

In the Epistles we see how the church became established and nourished itself on the word of the apostles. They had found new life in Christ; they had become a new community of faith. This was the Israel of God, the new nation, race, and priesthood. They had been called from darkness into light. Once they were no people, but now they were God's own people. Now they were called to proclaim Him who had called them (1 Pet. 2:9, 10).

For Further Study

Barclay, William. *The Mind of Jesus.* New York: Harper and Row, 1961.

Bruce, F. F. *The Spreading Flame.* Grand Rapids: Eerdmans, 1953.

Dentan, Robert C. *The Apocrypha*: *Bridge of the Testaments*. New York: Seabury Press, 1954.

Harrison, Everett F. *Introduction to the New Testament*. Grand Rapids: Eerdmans, 1964.*

Hunter, A. M. *Introducing the New Testament*. Philadelphia: Westminster Press, rev. ed., 1958.*

Kee, Howard Clark, and Young, Franklin W. *Understanding the New Testament*. Englewood Cliffs: Prentice-Hall, rev. ed., 1965.

Minear, Paul S. *The Gospel According to Mark*. Vol. 17 of *Layman's Bible Commentary*. Richmond: John Knox Press, 1962.*

Pfeiffer, Charles F. *Between the Testaments*. Grand Rapids: Baker Book House, 1959.

Tenney, Merrill C. *New Testament Times*. Grand Rapids: Eerdmans, 1965.*

Tenney, Merrill C. *New Testament Survey*. Grand Rapids: Eerdmans, rev. ed. 1961.*

---

*Recommended for the church library.

Chapter 4

Man Speaks of God's Work

Thus far we have sought to trace how man responded in faith and trust, and sometimes in disobedience, to the revelation of God. We have already said that revelation preceded the Scriptures. We must now add that the witness that man gave to this revelation also preceded the Scriptures.

We have always had the Bible in our homes and have become so accustomed to turning to it that we find it difficult even to imagine that there was a time when the Bible did not exist. But like all other literature, the books of the Bible had a beginning. In the next two chapters we want to look at how the Bible came into being. We will try to look at both the preliterary and literary forms of the development that resulted in what we now speak of as the Bible.

In our attempts to look at this material, we will follow the divisions of the Bible that the Hebrews followed; and that is reflected in the New Testament when it speaks of the law, the prophets, and the psalms (Lk. 24:44). To this we will then add the fourth division, the New Testament.

For convenience sake we will list the outline of the Old Testament books as they appear in this division, and they can then be compared with the division of the English Bible as it is usually given in the index of our Bibles.

I. *The Law*: Genesis, Exodus, Leviticus, Numbers, and Deuteronomy.

II. *The Prophets*
   1. The Former Prophets: Joshua, Judges, Samuel, and Kings. (The English Bible divides Samuel and Kings into two books each.)

2. Latter Prophets: Isaiah, Jeremiah, Ezekiel, and the twelve prophets.

III. *The Writings*: Psalms, Proverbs, Job, Song of Solomon, Ruth, Lamentations, Ecclesiastes, Esther, Daniel, Ezra, Nehemiah, and Chronicles.

What we will notice in these three divisions of the Bible as well as in the New Testament is that in each case there are a number of distinct stages of development in the formation of the Scriptures. There is first of all the original historical event in which the revelation is attested to or spoken of, then a period of oral tradition, a period of fragmentary accounts, and finally books and collections of books as we have them today. Let us observe this development in the sections already mentioned.

The Law

The origin and authorship of the Pentateuch (the first five books of the Old Testament) have been much discussed in recent years. Even to this day there is no unanimity on the subject. We will, therefore, need to state the particular theories involved and try to ascertain a few things that will be considered in the further discussion.

The traditional approach is that Moses wrote the first five books. Some who hold to Mosaic authorship allow that there may have been later redactions or editings, but others do not. This view claims basically that the first five books come substantially from the time of Moses and that he is the real author.

In the traditional view all the terms such as: "the law" (Ezra 10:3; Neh. 8:7, 9, 14; and Jn. 7:19), "the book of the law" (Neh. 8:3; Gal. 3:10), "the book of the law of Moses" (Neh. 8:1), "the books of Moses" (Neh. 13:1; 2 Chron. 25:4; 35:12; and Mk. 12:26), "the law of the Lord" (Ezra 7:10; 1 Chron. 16:40; and Lk. 2:23, 24), "the law of Moses" (Lk. 2:22; Jn. 7:23) are interpreted as referring to the Pentateuch, the written document.

The documentary theory of the origin of the Pentateuch suggests that there are four basic sources which lie behind the present five books. The earliest source known as the J source (because of its preference for Jahweh as the name for God) is dated around 950 B.C. The E source (because it uses Elohim as the name for God) is dated ninth or eighth century B.C. The D source which reflects the teachings of the Book of Deuteronomy is dated around 650 B.C. The latest source, P, is dated after 587 B.C., which is after the Exile and is generally held to represent the work of the priestly group in Israel.

The documentary theory holds that these four sources were woven together at various stages in the transmission of these materials. The present Pentateuch is then a composite of these sources. In this view the terms mentioned above, such as "the law of Moses" and "the book of the law of Moses," are held to refer to the Mosaic law as such or to particular parts of the Pentateuch written by Moses.

This is not the place to argue the relative merits of these two theories but it should be noted that it is possible to hold either one and yet not reject the authority of the Pentateuch as Holy Scripture.

What is more important for us at this point is to try to see how these materials came into being. *Several stages in the development of the Pentateuch* can be seen simply by looking at what we find in the text of the Bible itself.

1. *The first testimony.* First of all it is clear that the first testimony to the revelation of God is often given long before the written documentation. The first testimony was usually given at the time the revelation was received. Thus Jacob called the place where God appeared to him "Bethel" (Gen. 28:19, house of God), saying "this is none other than the house of God" (Gen. 28:17).

We can assume also that the songs of victory in Exodus 15 were sung at the occasion of the successful crossing of the Red Sea and thus were composed at least sometime before their incorporation into the Pentateuch, even if one were to assume Mosaic authorship.

When Jacob blesses his children we have a careful composition in poetic form of a message spoken years before it was included in the Scriptures (Gen. 49). This then is the primary witness to the revelation that these men received of God.

2. *Oral transmission.* What we have said thus far makes it only too evident that a second stage of transmission must be assumed to have existed between the original witness to God's revelation and its appearance in written form. This is often referred to as the period of oral transmission.

The art of writing was known in Israel prior to the day of Moses, but, until the time of David, writing played a fairly insignificant role and was confined largely to practical affairs. Thus the basic things of life such as the history of the tribe or the people, their songs of worship, and their sayings were committed to memory and transmitted orally (by word of mouth) from generation to generation rather than being preserved through writing.

In this way the tradition of what God had done in a series of mighty acts from the time of Abraham to Moses was transmitted orally until the time when it was finally written down.

It was undoubtedly through the medium of oral tradition that such items as the song of Lamech (Gen. 4:23f.) and of Heshbon and Sihon (Num. 21:27f.); the curses and blessings of Noah (Gen. 9:25-27), of Melchizedek (Gen. 14:19f.), of Rebekah (Gen. 24:60), etc., came down to the writer.

We who have not learned to use our faculty to memorize often become somewhat skeptical of this period of oral transmission and question the reliability of the material transmitted in this way; yet, in ancient times, memory was more reliable than the written account. Even today a child in his earliest years will detect the slightest change in a story he has come to know. We have many illustrations of the reliability of oral tradition where it is relied on by a whole people.

3. *Written fragments.* A third stage in the transmission of material is that in which fragments of the tradition appear in written form. Thus in the Pentateuch it is recorded that Moses was com-

manded at various times to write down specific laws. In this way the Book of the Covenant, which includes the Ten Commandments, was prepared (Ex. 24:4-7; 34:27). Another recognizable collection of laws is the Deuteronomic Code found in Deuteronomy 12-25, and a third is the so-called Laws of Holiness in Leviticus 17-26, which is a compilation of ritual and moral prescriptions, reflecting the struggle against Canaanite culture.

We have in the mentioning of the sites of Moab (Num. 21:14f.) an illustration of the quoting of another written source, the Book of the Wars of Jahweh. This book was not included in the canon but is referred to as a source used by the writer. It is also possible that some of the genealogies and materials of this type were written down in isolated fragments before being incorporated into the large corpus of materials.

4. *Compilation and composition.* The fourth stage in the growth of the Pentateuch is clearly that of compilation and composition. It is in this area where most of the disagreement has centered.

If Mosaic authorship is adhered to for the entire Pentateuch, then all of the work of compiling it out of the oral and written tradition has to be ascribed to Moses. To do so presents some real difficulties, not only with the last chapter of Deuteronomy which continues the history of Israel beyond Moses' death, but also with other parts of the account that seem to be colored by the later history of Israel. It also presents a problem with respect to language in that certain parts reflect the language of a later period of time.

The least that one would need to add would be an author for the last chapter of the Pentateuch and one or more editors or redactors, who later revised some of the original text. Thus, for example, in Genesis 14:14 Abraham pursued the captors of Lot as far as the city of Dan; yet, according to Judges 18:29, this place was not known by that name until long after the time of Moses.

The documentary theory which speaks to the same questions in a different way is not just a novel theory. It has arisen directly out of the problems encountered in the study of the Pentateuch itself. It holds that compilation of the oral and written traditions were made at different times in Israel's history and, therefore, also with different interest in mind. Still later these accounts were woven into one account with the separate compilations being lost.

This whole procedure should not be strange to us, for the work of Jesus, who in many ways was foreshadowed by Moses, is also described in four Gospels. Had the attempt of Tatian in the third century A.D. succeeded in welding the four Gospels into one continuous narrative, which he called the Diatessaron, and the four had been lost, then we would have had a parallel to the Pentateuch in the New Testament.

For our purposes it is enough to say that these two views of authorship demand the same kind of view of God's working in history. Mosaic authorship demands not only that another author added the last chapter to Deuteronomy, but also that the changes in the text made later in Israel's history by another editor were made under the inspiration of the Spirit of God. The documentary theory likewise requires the belief that later editors and compilers worked under the inspiration of the Spirit in giving us the Pentateuch.

The Prophets

It may be asked to begin with, why the Hebrews included Joshua, Judges, Samuel, and Kings with the prophets when we have normally regarded them as historical books. One reason may be that the historian in Israel was really not interested in history as such, not even the history of Israel. He was interested much more in penetrating the meaning of history. He saw the meaning of history as it related to God, the Sovereign Lord. It is likely because of this that these books are seen as belonging to the prophets who also helped to interpret history to the people.

Similarly, we could ask why the other historical books such as Chronicles, Ezra, Nehemiah, Ruth, and Esther are not listed with the former prophets and why Daniel is not listed with the latter prophets. The reason why all of these appear in the Writings is probably because they were being written and collected at a time when the Former and Latter Prophets were already being regarded as a unified body of materials.

The stages of growth in this material is similar to that of the law. In historical materials we have, of course, first and foremost the events themselves. These alone are of little interest to the writer. It is that event or that part of Israel's history that most clearly points to God's sovereignty and action that is chosen or lifted up in the witness.

The writer found the history preserved for him in the oral tradition of his day or in written documents such as the Wars of the Kings of Judah and the Wars of the Kings of Israel. These materials were then ordered and edited into a continuous whole.

The historical books are, therefore, written as a witness in themselves to the revelation of God. They lift up what God has done in the life of the nation.

Of all the Old Testament books, the Book of Jeremiah tells us most about its own origin and composition. This illustrates, in a general way at least, how some of the other prophetic books may have originated.

Jeremiah spoke his divine oracles against Israel before the beginning of Josiah's reign (*ca.* 621 B.C.). The Lord's command to write down these oracles did not come to Jeremiah until 604 B.C. The oracles that he wrote down included oracles that he had spoken over a period of twenty-three years (chapters 1-6). This tells us that these oracles, when originally spoken must have been in more concrete form than we have often supposed. Their poetic form also testifies to this fact.

When, in the time after the death of Josiah, Jeremiah again speaks out against his nation and advocates submission to Babylon, he reaps the displeasure of King Jehoiachim. On this occasion the king burns Jeremiah's writings. Jeremiah is instructed by the Lord to transcribe them again and Jeremiah again dictates his oracles for Baruch to write down. This time he adds new oracles to the ones originally written (Jer. 36:32).

Even when we take this additional material into account, there are reasons for believing that even more was added to the book at a later period. Thus the Greek translation of the book (LXX) is shorter than that of the Hebrew Bible. Furthermore, the Greek translation places chapters 44-51 after chapter 25:13, indicating that the way in which the fragments were ordered was not always the same.

From this study of the Book of Jeremiah we can assume that some, if not most, of the prophetic books went through the following four stages of development.

The first stage is the witness of the prophet as he speaks God's Word to a nation that has turned against God and is in political danger. It is a Word from God directed to an immediate situation (e.g., Amos speaking against the sins of Israel at Bethel).

The second stage is that of a period of oral tradition where the Word of God spoken by the prophet was transmitted or retained orally for a period of time, either by the prophet himself or by those who heard him.

The third stage is the time when these prophecies were written down and preserved in fragmentary form. Not all the prophetic books are unified compositions, as we have already seen.

The final stage was the collecting of the various oracles of a prophet and retaining them in a single book or corpus of materials. At times this collection of materials was made not with an eye to a single prophet but with an eye to one and the same type of materials, i.e., they would gather the prophetic oracles speaking to the same situation or theme into one book.

The above explains why there has been such a long argument over the question whether Isaiah is a unified book written by Isaiah, or whether it is a collection of oracles that are similar in nature but not necessarily from the same period of time nor necessarily by the same author. Even if the book should have a multiple authorship, it is no less God's Word than if it had a single author. The task of the scholar is not to try to prove one or the other true, but simply to decide on the basis of all the available evidence what actually happened.

Enough has been said for us to note that each prophet bore testimony to God's revelation in his own way. Each book retained for posterity also had its own historic development, even though we may, in most cases, not have enough information to describe the full process. But more than that, each writing was preserved because it was recognized as a Word from the God of Israel.

The Writings

An important difference between the Old Testament and the New Testament is the fact that the Old Testament has recorded man's response to God's revelation in the form of the Writings. The central part of these Writings is the Psalter to which belong Job, Lamentations, and the Psalms. They are songs of lament and praise of many different types. The second main type of response is contained in the Wisdom Literature. (To this belong the Proverbs, the Book of Ecclesiastes, and one strain of the Book of Job.)

We have indicated earlier that our biblical books are seen as a response or a witness to the revelation of God. What we have in the writings, especially the Psalms and Proverbs, is a response to God's revelation in life and worship. It is as if a window were opened in the sanctuary, and we can look in and listen to the praise and worship of the great congregation of Israel.

The Writings, especially the Psalms, give us a good indication of how Israel moved from spontaneous response to God's revelation to the songbook of the ages. The individual psalms were composed in response to specific situations in life. At one time it was a hymn for a special festival; at another time it was a confession of repentance, a prayer or a song of praise. They were composed at various times and by different people to suit different situations in life.

Later these psalms were gathered into small collections, so

45

that we have psalms of David, psalms of Asaph, and the songs of the Children of Korah. Since King David made it his special interest to gather this kind of literature, the collections are usually grouped under his name, even though not all the psalms were written by David.

The Proverbs, Ecclesiastes, and parts of the book of Job are another kind of response to God's revelation known as Wisdom Literature. It is an expression of common practical insight into life. We often call these short pithy sayings maxims. This literature is not closely tied to the historical events of God's special revelation; it is rather a bridge which indicates to the man who has accepted God's revelation that all the world, even its practical wisdom (today we might say science), belongs to God and is sacred. It must not be permitted to be separated from the life lived in obedience to God.

In this literature there is also the indication that the man of God is open to all people. There is an openness to other cultures and the words of wisdom from other nations have been admitted into the Book of Proverbs (Egypt, Arabia, and others). So also today, science needs to be open to all people for it is common to all men.

The Wisdom Literature even knows how man's search for truth often leads to a kind of skepticism. The Writings are well aware of the nihilistic, atheistic, or skeptical responses of men, and to have this type of response recorded in Ecclesiastes is no small comfort in the twentieth century.

The Writings are materials that cover almost the entire history of Israel. There are very early materials and very late materials. There is a direct address to God in praise and worship, but there is less of a claim made in the Writings to be sacred Scripture such as we found in the law or with respect to the prophets. It can be said that this is man's word to man (teaching) and man's word to God (praise and prayer) which has become God's Word to man.

For Further Study

Anderson, Bernhard W. *The Unfolding Drama of the Bible.* New York: Reflection Books, Association Press, 1957.

Goodspeed, Edgar J. *How Came the Bible?* New York: Abingdon Press, 1940.

Kuhl, Curt. *The Old Testament: Its Origins and Composition.* Richmond: John Knox Press, 1961. (Technical)

Rowley, Harold H. *The Growth of the Old Testament.* New York: Torchbooks, Harper and Row, 1963.

Trent, Robbie. *How the Bible Came to Us.* Nashville: Broadman Press, 1964. A children's book for grades four to seven.

Weiser, Artur. *The Old Testament: Its Formation and Development.* New York: Association Press, 1961. (Technical)

Chapter 5

From Copy to Canon

In the revelation of God in the New Testament we have the same sequence of events as in the Old Testament. First, there was God's self-revelation. This time revelation came through Jesus, the Son of God Incarnate. In Him the fullness of God was made manifest. The Gospels indicate how men responded in faith or unbelief to this revelation of God. This witness to the gospel is retained for us in the books of the New Testament.

The Gospels

Although the Gospels were not the first of the New Testament books to be written, they are correctly placed at the beginning of the New Testament canon since the witness to the gospel as contained in the four Gospels is everywhere assumed in the Epistles, even though these Gospels did not yet exist at the time when the Epistles were written.

In the New Testament as in the Old Testament, we need to become aware of the stages of growth of the books that have been collected for us. We will see here a close parallel to that of the Old Testament procedure.

The first stage in the events that led to the formation of the Gospels was undoubtedly the teaching of Jesus himself. We are told that the message "was declared at first by the Lord" (Heb. 2:3). We must not overlook how carefully Jesus taught His disciples during His earthly ministry. It is to be assumed, in that He allows himself to be called a Rabbi, that His method of teaching was similar to that of the Rabbis'. The Rabbis taught in such a way that a major teaching on a given subject would be reduced to one condensed pithy saying which the disciples (learners) had to memorize.

A good illustration of this can be seen in the Sermon on the Mount. Jesus spoke to both the crowd and the disciples (Mt. 5:1; 7:28). There was, in other words, a preaching and a teaching function performed almost simultaneously. What was proclaimed openly was probably taught to His disciples in short sayings, such as those we now have in the Sermon on the Mount.

The Gospels clearly indicate that Jesus accepted and underlined the authority of the Old Testament as the Word of God and openly appealed to it in His teaching (Mk. 10:17ff.; Lk. 24:44ff.; and Mt. 5:17). At the same time Jesus sees himself as the one who fulfills the law and as having authority in regard to the Old Testament. He decided what is God's unchanging Word and what part of the law is of a temporary functional character (Mt. 5:20f.; 15:1ff.). This lordship over the Scripture is best seen in Jesus' own teaching. Jesus came to fulfill the law, yet, where the Law of Moses had permitted divorce, Jesus did not hesitate to say that this was a concession to man's sin and should no longer be followed in the New Covenant (Mt. 5:27f.; 19:3ff.).

The extent to which the words of Jesus themselves became authoritative in New Testament times is reflected in the fact that even Paul, who had not been taught by Jesus personally, indicates to the Corinthians that on certain questions they have a word from the Lord (1 Cor. 7:10f.). This seems to settle the question. All of this indicates that the first stage in the growth and development of the Gospels was the life and ministry of Jesus Christ and His teaching, both before and after His death and resurrection.

The second stage of development was the stage of oral transmission of the tradition. It was in reality a period when the gospel was being preached to the people. It is only when we look at it from the standpoint of the development of the Gospels that we see it as a time when the sayings and words of Jesus, the accounts of His miracles and His teachings were retained in oral form.

This is reflected in the New Testament where Paul, who was not taught directly by Jesus, could quote words and teachings of Jesus that are not mentioned in the Gospels (Acts 20:35). Thus, for example, Paul quotes Jesus as saying, "Do this in remembrance of me" in instituting the Lord's Supper (1 Cor. 11:24). These words are not in the texts of the Gospels, but some of the later manuscripts add it to Luke 22:19. (See RSV.) The Apostle John also indicates that there were "many other things which Jesus did," but they could not all be written (Jn. 21:25).

The gospel tradition was, however, much more fixed than we may at first think when oral transmission is suggested. It had very specific content and form and not everyone could hand on a tradition received. This is the reason why Jesus taught the disciples and gave a special revelation of the gospel to Paul (Gal. 1:10-12). These became the guardians of the tradition under the guidance of the Holy Spirit. It was their task to pass on the tradition as they had received it (1 Cor. 15:3f.; 11:23; 11:2); and Paul could be very outspoken in denouncing any other tradition (Gal. 1:6-9).

There are also other indications that this gospel tradition was of relatively fixed content. Paul, who had not visited Rome before, assumes that the church at Rome has received the same gospel he has preached, both in doctrine and in ethics (Rom. 6:17; 16:17). It is indicated further that Paul's gospel was recognized by the other apostles (Gal. 2:7). Interestingly, Paul indicates that he did not receive the gospel from any of the apostles for he had been with the Apostle Peter for only two weeks. In other words, "to receive" the gospel meant much more than could be accomplished in that short a period of time. It could not be mastered or committed to memory in such a short time.

This much had to be said to indicate that the process of oral transmission was not a haphazard procedure open to errors and inaccuracies. It was, however, not fixed in the order of the accounts and teachings. This ordering of the material was done later. The apostles were the guardians of the tradition during this period of time for they were the primary witnesses to the works and words of Jesus. They could speak what they had seen and heard (1 Jn. 1:1ff.).

The stage of oral transmission was relatively short in the case of the Gospels when compared with the hundreds of years that often separated event and the record of the event in the Old Testament. In the New Testament, by the time the firsthand witnesses passed off the scene, the tradition was in written form. That it should be so, was already hinted at by Jesus himself.

In Judaism the tradition was handed down from rabbi to rabbi orally. When the disciple (follower or learner) had completely and accurately mastered the content of the tradition, he became a rabbi himself and began teaching others. But Jesus indicated that His disciples are not to be called rabbi (Mt. 23:7, 8). This is as much as to say that Jesus himself would remain the teacher for all time, and this is essentially what happened in that a new way was found to preserve the witness to the revelation received in Christ.

The third stage of the development of the New Testament materials was a period in which fragmentary writings of Jesus' work and sayings appeared and were preserved. In a time when the primary witnesses and guardians of the tradition were becoming fewer in number, more and more of the life and teaching of Jesus were committed to writing. By the time Luke wrote his Gospel he indicated that many had been writing accounts, even if fragmentary accounts, of the ministry of Jesus (Lk. 1:1-4).

The study of the Synoptic Gospels (Matthew, Mark, and Luke) indicates quite clearly that the Gospel of Mark or the source Mark used was available to Matthew and Luke when they wrote their Gospels. Besides this, however, it is also clear that Matthew and Luke both referred to another source (called Q for Quelle) in those areas in which these two Gospels differ from Mark, but agree with each other. In all likelihood it was a written source, because they follow the same order or sequence of materials.

The fourth stage of the development of the Gospels was the writing of the Gospels in their present form. Here, as always, life had preceded literature. It became increasingly important that the facts about Jesus should be set down in an orderly written account. This task was accomplished by the Gospel writers.

Each of the writers wrote with a specific purpose in mind. Luke even tells us to whom he is writing (Lk. 1:3). In all probability they also wrote to specific geographic areas (Matthew to Syrian-Palestine area; Mark to Rome, etc.). All of this was borne in mind when the writers chose out of the oral and written tradition available to them that which was best suited for the purposes they had in mind. As a result we have in the Gospels a richness and variety of information and yet an amazing agreement, not only in content but in outline and in form. It speaks for the authenticity of the events so recorded.

The Acts of the Apostles

Luke intended the Book of Acts to be a continuation of the Gospel, but the material is of a different nature. We can therefore take the introduction to Luke's Gospel as applying also to the Book of Acts. If this is correct then we can assume that the same stages of development hold for this part of his writings as we have observed in the Gospels.

It is obvious that the events recorded form the base of the writing. These have, however, been gathered from various sources. The writer at times identifies himself with certain accounts by using the personal pronoun *we* (Acts 16:10-17; 20:5—21:18; 27:1—28:16). These can be considered firsthand reports. Those parts where the third person pronoun (he, they) is used were possibly received through his association with Paul or the other apostles.

The Epistles

The Epistles represent a different type of literature altogether. They are not intent on giving us a careful record of the tradition as do the Gospels, yet, they everywhere presuppose this tradition. The Epistles are a record of the actual process of exhortation and teaching in the early church.

Many of the letters of Paul and Peter were written because of specific faults, dangers and/or needs that existed in the church. Paul wrote Galatians to guard against nullifying the gospel through legalism. Peter wrote his first letter to strengthen the church in a time of persecution. The letters to the Corinthians give us a good insight into the way the apostles spoke to the many, many problems encountered by the new churches.

In one sense the Epistles are like the Psalms in the Old Testament. The Psalms permit us to look in and see the great congregation of Israel at worship: the Epistles allow us to look in and see how the apostles exhorted and taught the Christian community on the basis of God's Word. In another way, they could be compared to the prophetic writings of the Old Testament. The prophets in their work called Israel back to keep the Covenant: the Epistles call the Christian community to be true to the gospel received. Since the apostles spoke as guardians of the gospel, they spoke with authority also on the meaning of the gospel for the life and conduct of the church. It is this kind of instruction that we find in the Epistles.

The stages of development of this part of the New Testament are different from that of the Gospels. Here we begin with the written letters of the apostles even though the writers undoubtedly used traditional material such as songs (Phil. 2:5-11) and benedictions and ethical precepts (1 Pet. 2:13—3:7) in their writings. In the Epistles we have the actual letters written to the churches.

The writers of these letters probably did not write with the intention of writing Holy Scripture. Nevertheless, they wrote to the churches with an authoritative word from the Lord and it is this that caused the church to value, guard, preserve, and collect their writings.

The second stage of development was then the actual preserving and collecting of these letters. Some of the letters were clearly meant to be read in a whole circuit of churches (1 Pet. 1:1), and each church no doubt retained a copy of it for its own keeping. As questions arose on other subjects, they no doubt tried to find letters written to other churches which might prove helpful. In any case, we have evidence that very early in the life of the church the writings of Paul had been collected and were known throughout the church (2 Pet. 3:15).

The Book of Revelation

The Book of the Apocalypse of John is the only book of its kind in the New Testament. Characteristic of this type of literature is the thought that God is sovereign and that God in the end will intervene in the events of time and in a cataclysmic or violent fashion bring about His goodwill.

The book was written to encourage the church as it was about to face severe persecution. It points to the ultimate victory of Christ over sin and death in spite of what might look to the human eye as a victory of sin and Satan at the present moment.

The Recognition of the Books as Scripture

A. The Old Testament

Thus far we have not mentioned a very essential stage of development in both the Old and New Testament literature—the recognition of these writings as sacred Scripture. How the Bible came to have unique authority involves the discussion of the canon of the Bible. The *Canon* is the list of books accepted by the church as genuine and inspired Holy Scripture. Such recognition was not accorded to all sections of the Bible at the same time. It will thus be helpful to discuss it under the divisions of the Hebrew Canon and the New Testament.

The Law. The Law was already recognized as having divine authority at the time when God made His Covenant with Israel (Ex. 24). God had commanded Moses to write the Book of the Covenant. These words were read in the covenant ceremony and the people promised to do all the words of the Lord.

This same recognition is given also to the rest of the Pentateuch in that Moses exhorts his people not to add or subtract anything from the commandments of God (Deut. 4:2; 12:32). There is thus an emphasis on the authority of the Law to be seen in the Pentateuch itself.

The internal evidence is confirmed by later testimony from other parts of Scripture. The Law was highly esteemed at the time of Ezra and Nehemiah. They accorded the Law of Moses a position above all other writings. They studied it diligently and read and expounded it to the people (Ezra 7:10; Neh. 8:8). In all likelihood the *Law* by this time referred to the whole Pentateuch or at least to the whole Mosaic tradition. By New Testament times there was, of course, no doubt of the basic authority of the books of Moses for the Law is always mentioned first (Lk. 24:44).

The Prophets. The Prophets spoke and wrote with authority. They were aware of their commission to speak for God and wherever they went they spoke with an emphatic "thus saith the Lord." But we may question whether they as individual speakers and writers were fully aware of the fact that they were "adding" to the sacred Scriptures which was expressly forbidden in the Law (Deut. 4:2).

The reason why these new writings could be added to the Law was likely that they did not bring in anything new, in the sense of being contrary to the old. What the prophets did was to make explicit what was intended by the Law. The prophets tried to spell out the implication of the Law and exhorted and warned the people on the basis of the Covenant. Seeing that Israel had broken the Covenant they also pointed to a time when God would make a new Covenant with His people.

It is not surprising to find, therefore, a recognition of the canonicity of earlier prophetic works by the later prophets who saw the significance of these works. Zechariah places the unpopular word of the prophet on a par with the law when he says, "They made their hearts like adamant lest they should hear the law *and* the words which the Lord of hosts had sent by his Spirit through the former prophets" (Zech. 7:12).

Similarly, the Book of Daniel, which in this division belongs to the Writings (See chap. 4.), twice refers to the prophets as servants of God (Dan. 9:6, 10) which is a technical designation

55

going back to Moses. Thus long before the time of the New Testament the Prophets were regarded as sacred Scripture.

The Writings. The Writings in contrast to the Law and the Prophets make much less explicit claims to divine authority. This is no doubt related to the type of material that they represent.

There was likely little difficulty in accepting as canonical the historical books in the Writings because they paralleled and extended the work of the former prophets. In like manner, the Psalms were the hymnbook of the congregation. These Writings were simply a part of the life of the people and received their authority in this way.

In the intertestamental period the grandson of Jesus Ben Sira refers (*ca.* 132 B.C.) in the prologue to his grandfather's book, Ecclesiasticus, to the "Law, Prophets, and other books." "Other books" here refers at least to the Writings, but it may also have included the books of the Apocrypha.

We have already mentioned Jesus' reference to "Law, Prophets, and Psalms" where all the Writings are no doubt included. That Jesus was aware of the extent of the Old Testament canon seems to be indicated in His reference to the Old Testament history as extending from Abel to Zechariah (Mt. 23:35; Lk. 11:51); the first chosen from Genesis and the second from Chronicles, the last book in the Hebrew canon. Oddly enough, Jesus often quotes the Psalms or Isaiah when speaking about the "law" (Jn. 10:34; 12:34; 15:25) as did Paul also (1 Cor. 14:21). In this sense the term *law* becomes synonymous with the Old Testament Scriptures.

B. The New Testament

The writings of the New Testament other than the Gospels consisted of very casual writings. There seems to have been no conscious human design for the preparation of the New Testament. But it was the purpose of God to give us this witness to His revelation of himself in Christ Jesus.

To be sure, there are a few references by New Testament writers that indicate the divine origin and authority of the message that they have proclaimed and of that which they wrote (1 Cor. 2:6-13; Rev. 1:1-3). Peter places the epistles of Paul on the level of other Scripture (2 Pet. 3:15), and the apostles expected their letters to be read in all the churches. They were therefore not ordinary letters and were received from the beginning as being of special worth.

As early as A.D. 95 Clement of Rome quotes freely not only from the Old Testament but also from Matthew, Luke, Romans, Corinthians, Hebrews, Timothy, 1 Peter, Titus, and Ephesians. Polycarp in A.D. 110 refers to ten of Paul's letters. By A.D. 150 Tatian attempted to weave the four Gospel accounts into one continuous narrative about the life of Christ. By the time of Justin in the middle of the second century, the Gospels were already used publicly on par with the Old Testament.

The first clear evidence of the process of canonization comes, however, from Marcion who rejected the Old Testament and accepted only the Gospel of Luke and some of Paul's letters (excluding the pastoral epistles) as canonical. The Muratorian Canon (A.D. 150 or somewhat later) was set up to oppose the heresy of Marcion and gives us an idea which books of the New Testament were accepted beyond dispute in the early church. It is the first document concerned specifically with listing the books belonging to the New Testament. All the books of the New Testament are listed except Hebrews, 1 and 2 Peter, and James, but it also lists two books which were later rejected: the wisdom of Solomon and the Apocalypse of Peter.

Origen in the third century accepted the twenty-seven books which we now have in the New Testament. Nevertheless, he expressed some doubts about Hebrews, James, Peter, and 2 and 3 John.

Eusebius of Caesarea had to prepare fifty Bibles for the churches in Constantinople. After careful study of the question he included our present twenty-seven books, noting however that James, 2 Peter, 2 and 3 John, and Revelation were still being disputed by some.

At the Council of Carthage in A.D. 397 a formal ratification of the present twenty-seven books was given by the entire church. Since Jerome in translating the Bible into Latin in the fifth century used these twenty-seven books, the decision for all practical purposes was made for all time, since the later versions and translations go back to the Latin Vulgate.

The whole process of the canonization of the New Testament took about three hundred years. It was no simple matter to decide which books were authentic and which were not. Criteria used by the church in determining which books should be retained could be listed as follows:

1. Do the books have apostolic authority? They had to be either the works of apostles or persons who were in a position to have been corrected by apostles, as for example, Luke and Mark.

2. The reception of the writings by the original churches and the continued knowledge and use of the writings by subsequent generations. This criterion was simply applying the test of time and relevance to the writings. As a result it is possible that even some of the letters of the apostles may not have been retained.

3. Consistency of doctrine with the standard recognized in the Old Testament and in the tradition of the New Testament.

On the basis of standards used by the church, books such as the Didache (Teaching of the Twelve Apostles), the Epistles of Clement, the Shepherd of Hermas, the Gospel According to the Hebrews, the Gospel of Peter, the Gospel of Nicodemus, and the Acts of Pilate, Peter, John, Andrew, Thomas and Paul and many other books were excluded from the canon.

The Inspiration of Scripture

There is no doubt but that the testimony of Scripture is that the Scriptures were inspired of God. Paul says "all Scripture is inspired by God" (2 Tim. 3:16). It means literally "God breathed" Scripture. In this way it is recognized that God ultimately is the author of Scripture.

Peter says that those who prophesied were men who were empowered by the Spirit to speak a God-given message and in like manner, those who interpret it must be empowered by the same Spirit (2 Pet. 1:20, 21).

These two references should help us to avoid several errors that are often made when considering the question of inspiration. The first is that we should avoid limiting inspiration to the inspiration of the writer at the point of writing. We should rather apply the concept of inspiration to all the stages of development as we have observed them. The original witness to the revelation and its final record were alike inspired by the Spirit.

Notice that 2 Timothy 3:16 does not say the writer was inspired. He says all Scripture is inspired. Similarly, 2 Peter 1:20ff. says that the prophecy spoken by the prophet came by the Spirit of God. This should be taken to refer to both the prophet's original message and its record in Scripture. Since these two were often separated by many years it stands to reason that the activity of the Holy Spirit is seen in the whole process, not only one segment of it.

Thus the Spirit of God was active in opening men's hearts and minds to the revelation of God; He was active also in empowering men to give a witness to the revelation he had received. Beyond this the Holy Spirit was active in guarding over the witness to this revelation in the period of its oral transmission. Equally, the Holy Spirit inspired men to preserve, collect, write down, and order the witness received. He inspired a David and a Solomon to write and to collect Psalms and Proverbs just as much as He inspired Peter and Paul to write their letters to the churches. Above all, the Holy Spirit was active in the great congregation of Israel and in the church, guiding in the recognition of those books which should be received into the canon of Scripture. To see how God worked in history to give us His Word makes us marvel anew at the greatness of God.

Later we will have occasion to speak about the transmission of the text of the Bible from the time of its writing to the present. But we can point out here that the Spirit of God also guarded the text of Scripture over all these centuries.

It is on the basis of what God has done in the past that we

today have the firm conviction that God by His Spirit will also now watch over His Word. Even now when the Bible is being translated into a thousand languages (and no translation gives exactly the sense of the original), we can have the confidence that the Word of God will abide. We can safely take to heart in this respect the counsel of Gamaliel "if this plan or this undertaking is of men, it will fail; but if it is of God, you will not be able to overthrow them. You might even be found opposing God!" (Acts 5:38, 39). So also a translation that does not serve God's purpose any longer will not stand the test of time. Our confidence in the present ministry of the Spirit makes alarmed Bible-burning unnecessary.

For Further Study

Bruce, F. F. *The New Testament Documents: Are They Reliable?* Grand Rapids: Eerdmans, 1954.

Bruce, F. F. *The Books and the Parchments.* Westwood: Fleming H. Revell Co. rev. ed.

Filson, Floyd V. *Which Books Belong in the Bible?* Philadelphia: Westminster Press, 1957.*

Metzger, Bruce Manning. *The New Testament: Its Background, Growth, and Content.* New York: Abingdon Press, 1965.*

---

*Recommended for the church library.

Chapter 6

From Text to Translation

We want to give some attention now to the way in which the text of Scripture was written, preserved, and passed on to succeeding generations. This will also include the translation of the Bible into many languages.

The Writing of Manuscripts

A. Languages Used

Writing as such is an ancient art. No one knows exactly when it was invented. The first system for which we have evidence was probably created by the Sumerians (Mesopotamians) around 3300 B.C. Thus, long before Moses, much literature, religious and otherwise, had already been produced, and a variety of scripts were in use throughout the Ancient Near East.

When Abraham and his family came to Palestine (*ca.* 2000 B.C.), the Canaanites, or Phoenicians, also had an alphabet and a literature all their own. Recent discoveries at Ugarit in Syria have helped us to know more about the writings and religious beliefs of that time.

Most of the Old Testament was first written in the Hebrew language (cf. Is. 19:18 "the language of Canaan"). It belongs to the Semitic language family which includes Assyrian, Phoenician, Babylonian, Arabic, Syriac, and others. We are not surprised then, to find that the Hebrew and Phoenician alphabets are in fact quite closely related.

The Hebrew alphabet of twenty-two letters is made up of consonants only. The vowels were simply "read in" by those who knew them. The Bible in our language would then begin with Genesis 1:1 as follows:

HTRHTDNSNVHHTDTRCDGGNNNGBHTN (←Read this way.)

Sentences were written from right to left and a document began at the last page of the book as we would read it. Early manuscripts were written mainly in the square letters one finds in any Hebrew Bible today.

A few shorter sections of the Old Testament were written in Aramaic (Dan. 2:4b—7:28 and Ezra 4:8—6:18 and 7:12-26, as well as some isolated words in other books). The Aramaic language is also a member of the Semitic family and was at first spoken primarily in Syria. After the eighth century B.C., it became the diplomatic language of the Assyrian Empire and came to be used in the Persian Empire as well. While in exile, the Israelites learned the Aramaic language and after returning to Palestine and finding they had forgotten the Hebrew, they continued to use the Aramaic as their own language.

Aramaic expressions are found also in the New Testament. Such words as *Abba* meaning "father" (Mk. 14:36); *Maranatha*, i.e., "Our Lord, come" (1 Cor. 16:22); and the saying of Jesus on the cross, "Eloi, Eloi, lama sabachthani" (Mk. 15:34) are some of the best known examples. It is thought that Aramaic was the customary language of our Lord and His apostles, as well as the early Palestinian church.

The New Testament authors, however, wrote mainly in Greek, the common language of their day. Because it belongs to the Indo-European language family, it is more closely related to English and German. New Testament Greek is sometimes called Hellenistic or *koine* which indicates a stage of development later than the classical period, i.e., the period from 300 B.C. to A.D. 500. Although scholars preferred the classical form of the language, the common people used the *koine*.

B. Materials Used

The Mesopotamians wrote mostly on tablets of clay, but other materials such as bone, stone, wood, metal, cloth, and especially parchment and papyrus were used as well. In biblical studies we are interested mainly in the latter two types of material, since most of the manuscripts of the Bible were probably written on parchment or papyrus.

Papyrus (from which we get our word *paper*) was made from the papyrus plant which grew plentifully in the Nile Valley, as well as in other marshy places. Its long stalks were cut into sections and then sliced into thin strips which were laid side by side vertically and horizontally and then pressed together to make a writing surface.

Parchment was manufactured from the skins of cattle, sheep, goats, and antelopes, particularly from their young. A superior kind of parchment was called vellum. It was more durable than papyrus which was easily subject to decay when it got wet. On the other hand, papyrus was thought to be easier for reading, because its writing surface was not as shiny as parchment.

Although papyrus was used as early as 3500 B.C. in Egypt, it became most common after the third century A.D. It is quite certain that the New Testament originals were written on such material. However, very few papyrus documents have survived except in the dry sands of Egypt. The Jews of later times preferred vellum for Scripture writing.

Publications commonly appeared in one of two forms: the scroll and the codex. Scrolls were made of either papyrus or parchment, and as we see in the Dead Sea Scrolls, even of metal. Sheets of material were glued or sewed together in long strips and wound around a stick at each end. One of these rolls might contain several biblical books. The scroll was hard to handle, since it had to be unwound with one hand and wound with the other while reading. They were also bulky for storing.

The early Christians popularized the codex. It was made by folding one or several sheets of papyrus or parchment in the middle and sewing them together along the folded edge. The result was a book similar to our books today.

The script usually was written in narrow parallel columns two to three inches wide. Before the tenth century A.D. Greek codices were generally written in capital or block letters called uncials.

Cursive script or writing was used primarily for nonliterary materials like letters. From this developed what is known as the minuscule or small-letter style which was also thought to be suitable for books and literature, at least after the tenth century when minuscules replaced the use of uncials.

The Scribes and Their Problems

The task of preserving the Scriptures was given to the scribes. It is obvious that this was no easy assignment. All copying was done by hand (the word *manuscript* comes from two Latin words *manu* and *scriptus* meaning "hand" and "writing"). They copied the manuscripts one at a time, but on occasion a dictation method in a scriptorium was used. Here a group of scribes would listen to dictation from a manuscript and then copy what they heard. In this way a number of books could be produced simultaneously.

It was very difficult to reproduce the material accurately by hand. Reading itself presented certain problems. The uncial codices were written without accents, punctuation, or spacing between words. John 1:1 would therefore appear something like this: INTHEBEGINNINGWASTHEWORDANDTHEWORDWA SWITHGOD. . . . Faulty divisions of words were therefore not unknown. If the handwriting was poor, it was hard to distinguish letters similar to each other, (cf. our *a* and *o*).

Some scribes would use abbreviations which a copyist would not understand and could duplicate incorrectly. When we read the old manuscripts we find that sometimes words or even whole lines were omitted. This happened if two consecutive lines ended with the same word; and as a scribe came to the end of the first line, and looked away, he might return to the end of the second line and leave out everything in between. Occasionally a word was written twice, when it should appear only once. The opposite also happened—that a word to be written twice was copied only once.

There could be errors of hearing as well. A lapse of attention or noise disturbance could easily result in mistakes. As a writer in the scriptorium listened to the reading he might hear a word but substitute another which sounded the same (cf. our words *hear* and *here*).

There is evidence also of intentional changes. Some scribes had peculiar spelling habits which could result in changing a text. Grammatical corrections were made at times to improve the literary style. Occasionally scribes would try to harmonize the wording of two similar passages, and thus make certain changes. When markings occurred in the margin, a scribe might decide to incorporate it in the text if it somehow seemed to fit in.

It is therefore not surprising that through the copying of manuscripts from one century to another, variations and changes did occur. Indeed, it is a wonder, one could say a miracle, that there are not many more. Actually, it is clear that the scribes were for the most part as careful as was humanly possible. The Jewish scribes particularly took almost infinite pains to insure the accuracy of their work.

The Manuscripts We Have

Although the original manuscripts of the books of the Bible are not in existence, thousands of manuscripts, either of the entire Bible or portions thereof, are available to us today. The Greek manuscripts of the New Testament (many of them just fragments of the text) total nearly 4700. Of these 240 or more are in the uncial script, and over 2500 are written in minuscule style. Almost 2000 Greek lectionaries exist also, i.e., groupings of Scripture passages suited to particular occasions of worship in the church. There are more than seventy papyri fragments as well, the other manuscripts being in the main of parchment material.

For the Old Testament some of the best manuscripts come from the Dead Sea collection, for example, an incomplete scroll of Isaiah (called B) as well as a complete scroll of that book (Isaiah A). Both are believed to have been written about two hundred years before Christ. From the same period comes a Hebrew manuscript of the Ten Commandments known as the Nash Papyrus. Other good manuscripts include a codex of the Prophets from about A.D. 900 and one of the entire Old Testament, dating from the first decade of the eleventh century. Both of these are kept at a Leningrad library in Russia today.

Several famous Greek codices of the New Testament might be mentioned as well.

1. *Codex Vaticanus* (B) is generally thought to be the most important and is kept at the Vatican Library in Rome. It dates from the fourth century A.D. It is written on vellum, but some sections of the New Testament are missing (e.g., the Pastoral Epistles, Philemon, and Revelation).

2. *Codex Sinaiticus* (Aleph) was found at Mount Sinai from which it gets its name. It is now in the British Museum and has been dated from the early fourth century A.D., perhaps a little later than B.

3. *Codex Alexandrinus* (A) is also lodged in the British Museum. It is fairly complete and belongs to the fifth century A.D. It is particularly helpful in the section of Revelation where other manuscripts are often incomplete.

4. *Codex Ephraemi Syri* (C) is located in Paris and belongs to the fifth century. It is a palimpsest, the original text of Scripture having been erased to make room for the sermons of Ephraem the Syrian. It is, however, possible to decipher the original text of Scripture even though it has been erased and written over.

5. *Codex Bezae* (D) is a fifth- or sixth-century manuscript now housed in Cambridge, England. It has the Greek of the Gospels and the Acts, together with a Latin translation.

Important because they frequently come from a time even earlier than these codices, are the papyri, especially the Chester Beatty collection. These are only small fragments which come from the Gospels, Epistles, and Revelation. A recently published fragment called P[66] or Bodmer II which covers John's Gospel, is dated around A.D. 200.

As was mentioned, the work of textual criticism is that of comparing all these manuscripts and trying to find the correct reading of the text. The number of manuscripts available is large and is constantly growing. The scholar collates (compares) these manuscripts in order to establish which of the variant readings is the correct one.

Through the years a method of study has been worked out to help scholars make decisions on which reading is to be preferred. A basic question is, Which of several different readings would most likely be the correct one if one considered the vocabulary, thought patterns, and general background of the author? Another question is, In view of the habits (and weaknesses) of scribes as we know them, which reading is more likely to have been the original one?

In the latter case, three principles are used as a rule of thumb:

1. A shorter reading is usually preferred to a longer one, because it is more likely that a scribe would have added than that he would have subtracted from the wording.

2. Harder readings are usually preferred to easier ones, because scribes would more readily smooth out a difficult reading than make a simple reading more difficult.

3. That reading is preferred which best explains the variations in the other manuscripts.

If a document has been proved many times to have the best readings, its testimony is highly regarded; and its text will be set aside for another only if the evidence against it is clear and overwhelming. Codices Aleph and B are regarded as good manuscripts for this reason.

Sometimes it is hard to be certain about the best reading, and in some cases, though these are rather rare, scholars may even need to make an intelligent guess because several readings could be considered with equal merit.

Textual criticism is an important work; and as more manuscripts are found and better methods of study are developed, this search for the correct text must continue.

As God's people faced their responsibility of proclaiming the gospel, they had to consider the question of translating the Bible into other languages. In this way many different versions and translations have come into existence and are being used today.

Already in the third century B.C. Greek-speaking Jews decided to translate the Old Testament into Greek, and the Septuagint (LXX) came into being. It included some books not found in the Old Testament, so not all Jews accepted it; but it was very widely circulated in the Mediterranean world. Other Greek translations were made several hundred years later. The quotations from the Old Testament in the New Testament indicate that the apostles may well have used the LXX translation. Another effort to help those who did not know the Hebrew was the preparation of the Aramaic Targums in which the Old Testament text was paraphrased in the Aramaic language for those who felt more at home in the Aramaic.

As early as the second century A.D. the Greek New Testament was also translated into other languages. The Diatesseron (Gospels in Syriac) has already been mentioned. A more polished translation into Syriac produced in the fourth century A.D. was called the Peshitta. Syriac-speaking Christians use it to this day. During that same period, a great missionary, Ulfilas, helped to translate the New Testament and most of the Old Testament into the language of the Goths.

A most important translation of the early centuries was the Latin Vulgate, prepared by Jerome. Although there had been earlier translations into Latin, they were rough and literalistic. Jerome, an outstanding scholar of the fourth Christian century, was asked by Damasus, the bishop of Rome, to make a standard Latin version for the use of the Western churches. This version has been used as the official text or Bible by the Roman Catholic Church.

Other early translations included the Coptic (third century A.D.), Ethiopic (fourth century A.D.), and the Arabic (seventh century A.D.). The evangelization of Armenia, Georgia, Nubia, and Bulgaria, as well as other nearby regions, made translations in these languages necessary as well.

The English Bible

In our own setting, the history of the English Bible might be given special attention. Earliest translations into English were made from the Latin Vulgate. Scholars like the Venerable Bede and Alfred the Great helped provide Anglo-Saxon translations of the Psalms and the Gospel of St. John in the eighth and ninth century A.D.

The first complete translation into English can be traced back to the work of John Wycliffe and his helper, John Purvey. Their work, dated in the latter part of the fourteenth century, circulated in manuscript only. Not before 1526 was the first English translation of the New Testament from the original Greek available. The translator was William Tyndale who was prevented from completing the Old Testament when he was burned at the stake on October 6, 1536.

The work of Miles Coverdale is renowned for being the first complete English Bible to be printed. The year was 1535. In the years that followed several important revisions were undertaken. In 1539 the Great Bible appeared, a copy of which was placed in every church in England under King Henry VIII's directive: "In God's name, let it go abroad among our people!" Perhaps even more significant was the Geneva Version issued in 1557 and destined to go through two hundred editions or more between 1560 and 1630. Shakespeare, John Bunyan, and the Pilgrim Fathers all used this Bible. Its scholarship was of the highest caliber. For many people it could not be replaced either by the Bishops' Bible of 1568 or the Authorized Version of 1611.

In fact, however, the publication of the Authorized Version, better known as the King James Version was a landmark in the history of the English Bible. This new version was urged by scholars for several reasons: 1) The English language had undergone many changes in the past fifty years; 2) Hebrew and Greek scholarship had been much improved during this same period; and 3) For various reasons earlier versions were not finding universal acceptance.

The work was begun in 1607 and was finished four years later. Of the English revisions in the Reformation period, it was the last, the best, and the most popular, finally superseding all the rest.

It should be mentioned perhaps, that the King James Version did not find universal acceptance either. Some received it with cold indifference and others with violent opposition. Through the ensuing decades some minor corrections were made, together with changes in spelling, punctuation, and use of capital letters to bring it into line with current practice.

Its worthiness and usefulness is possibly best attested to by the fact that no major revision was undertaken till the nineteenth century. In 1885 the complete Revised Version was published in England. Its counterpart, the American Standard Version (also called ARV), was published in America about twenty years later. It had made use of an older and better Greek text and had also corrected errors of translation in the King James Version. Many felt, however, that its style was stiff, lacking the dignity and vitality of its famous predecessor, the King James Version. As a result, the King James Version continued in use.

A recently completed major revision is the Revised Standard Version (RSV) issued in the New Testament in 1946 and in the Old Testament in 1952. The need for a revision this time was based on: 1) Discovery of new and better manuscripts (including the Chester Beatty papyri); 2) New information regarding the use of the biblical languages; 3) More available background material for a fuller understanding of the life and history of the Jewish people; and 4) Inferior literary style of the American Standard Version. The translators were instructed to make the most accurate translation possible, while at the same time seeking to recover the simplicity, the directness, the literary beauty, and the spiritual power of the King James Version.

As in the case of its ancestor, the King James Version, the Revised Standard Version, too, was severely criticized when it first appeared. Its strengths are its straightforward rendering of the English language and its high quality translation, using the latest manuscripts available, including the Dead Sea Scrolls. It is not perfect, and no doubt will continue to come under revision in the years to come.

Finally, mention must be made of the New English Bible the New Testament of which appeared in 1961. The contribution that it makes is that it is not a revision of any previous Bible. It is a direct translation of the Hebrew and the Greek texts. As a result, its translation differs markedly from previous translations but also has the possibility of being more true to the sense of the original text.

No mention has been made of literally dozens of other Protestant, Jewish, and Catholic translations. It might, however, be in place to indicate that, by and large, private translations as e.g., Phillips, Williams, Moffatt, or paraphrastic translations as e.g., *Living Letters* or *The Amplified Bible* should be used largely for study purposes.

The church must present the gospel to all nations, but many peoples have not yet heard His Word. The process of transmission and translation must therefore go on, so that the lives of others, too, may be filled and enriched. The church dare not be content with the work of previous generations, but must continue to seek a more faithful and meaningful rendering of the Holy Scriptures in man's words.

For Further Study

Bruce, F. F. *The Books and the Parchments*. Westwood: Fleming H. Revell, Co. rev. ed.

Bruce, F. F. *Second Thoughts on the Dead Sea Scrolls*. Grand Rapids: Eerdmans, rev. ed. 1961.

Bruce, F. F. *The English Bible*: *A History of Translations*. New York: Oxford University Press, 1961.*

Foreman, Kenneth J., et al. *Introduction to the Bible.* Vol. 1 of *Layman's Bible Commentary.* Richmond: John Knox Press, 1959.

Kenyon, Frederick. *Our Bible and the Ancient Manuscripts.* London: Eyre and Spottiswode, 5th rev. ed. 1958 or ed. by A. W. Adams, New York: Harper and Row, 1958.

Kenyon, Frederick. *The Text of the Greek Bible.* Naperville: Allenson, rev. ed. 1958.

Twilley, L. D. *The Origin and Transmission of the New Testament.* Grand Rapids: Eerdmans, 1958.

Vagany, Leo. *An Introduction to the Textual Criticism of the New Testament.* London: Sands & Company, 1937.*

---

*Recommended for the church library.

Chapter 7

The Bible Speaks to Us

God spoke in times past through His prophets and when the time was fully come, through His Son. He now speaks to us through His Word and the Spirit of God. We have seen earlier that it was precisely for this reason that a record of God's revelation to man was retained by Israel and by the church. It is now through this record that God confronts modern man with the revelation of himself in Christ.

God's manifestation of himself was given in specific events and related to specific circumstances in which men lived. There was always a human context in which God's Word became alive and relevant to man. It is no less so today. If the Bible does not speak to our own situation and to our own problems, then in effect it has nothing to say to us.

Looking back from the standpoint of the New Testament times, we can see that the Law, the Prophets, and the Writings were the Bible of Israel. These Scriptures were an authoritative guide for faith and practice. The Old Testament was to Israel what the Bible is to us today. But somehow we have gained the impression that the Bible has little to say to questions of the space age, and so we do not readily turn to the Bible for guidance and instruction in questions that relate to everyday life in the twentieth century.

One of the first things we must learn is that we cannot use the Bible as a vendor, putting in a nickel and expecting to have automatic delivery of goods. But this is what so many people expect to find. They give the Bible a few shakes, but, when nothing much comes of it, they conclude that the Bible has nothing to say to them.

Many people feel that the Bible does not speak to them, because they take a false approach to it, or bring to it false expectations. Such false approaches that could nullify for us the relevance of the Scriptures are many in number!

1. The Bible is not relevant to anyone who does not hear in these writings the Word of God. Those who do not respond to the message of the gospel do not have the Spirit of God who makes the Scriptures alive to them.

2. For anyone who brings to the Scriptures a spirit of legalism, either in doctrine or ethics, the Bible will not long yield its fruit. The Bible is not a rule book giving patent answers for every conceivable situation; it does not give to us a prescribed set of beliefs to which we must subscribe. The Bible calls us much more into a living relationship of faith and obedience to Jesus Christ, the Living God.

3. We cannot take a one-to-one approach to the Scriptures and find help. That is to say, we cannot look up the term *Labor Union* in the concordance; and, if the word does not appear in the Bible, assume that the Bible has nothing to say about our relationship to labor unions. Though the external problems of the present life situation are not the same as those in New Testament times, the Bible speaks to problems that man faces today.

4. We can also come to the Bible with the expectation that in reading the Bible we shall be strangely warmed inside, uplifted and inspired, sensing somehow the nearness of God. There is no doubt that the Bible can do this, but this is not its primary objective. Its primary objective is to help us to face life under the lordship of Christ and to help us to be obedient to the Lord's command, even though in our situation it might mean persecution or suffering. At no time should we use the Bible as a way of escape from the reality of the situation in which we live.

The way in which the Bible speaks to us can best be seen by looking at the way in which it spoke to the early Christians. Even though the Christians did not yet have the Bible in its completed form as we have it today, they essentially had the New Testament in what we have called the tradition, that is, that which the

Apostle Paul says that they have received from the Lord (1 Cor. 15:3f.). We can, therefore, see what the Scriptures meant to them and how the tradition related to their life. To see how the Word spoke to them may have some possibilities for us also.

The Tradition

Tradition (*paradosis*) in the New Testament would be roughly equivalent to what we have today in the Bible. It is that which is given, that which has been received. The New Testament writers distinguished two separate parts in the tradition—preaching and teaching. They distinguished these two both in their own work and in the ministry of Jesus.

A. Preaching (*Kerygma*)

Preaching had to do with proclaiming the good news. Three basic words were used to describe this activity: 1) *Euangelizesthai,* to preach good tidings; 2) *katangellion,* to declare or announce; and 3) *keryssein,* to proclaim or to herald. The fundamental idea is the telling of news to people who had not heard it before, or to evangelize. In the New Testament *preaching* has nothing to do with the delivery of sermons to the converted; it always means the proclamation of the gospel to the non-Christian world.

When we ask, What do these heralds proclaim? then we are asking a question about the content of their message or what is known as the *kerygma*. The kerygma is essentially the apostolic gospel—the message of the life, death, and resurrection of Christ. It speaks of the divine offer of life in Christ and the proclamation of the will of God for all mankind. The kerygma is not only a biography of Jesus' life; it is a saving message which God addresses to the whole world in Jesus Christ, the Living Word. Kerygma corresponds in the Old Testament to the various commandments and promises or offers of God's grace. The kerygma is both a divine offer and a divine appeal. It is a divine offer of the forgiveness of sins through the atoning work of Jesus Christ; it is an appeal for man to accept such forgiveness. Wherever, there-

75

fore, the Scriptures speak of the facts that are regarded as essential for salvation, you have kerygma.

B. Teaching (Didache)

Teaching, according to the New Testament, has to do with speaking to Christians—teaching them to observe all that Christ has commanded. Teaching is the message of God's Word directed to Christians. In the New Testament, teaching has to do with ethical instruction and sometimes with instruction in the faith. Teaching is concerned with man's proper response of obedience to the will of God. It corresponds to Torah or the law in the Old Testament—authoritative instruction concerning what man ought to do and to know. The teaching (didache) goes back to Jesus as does the preaching (kerygma).

The teaching is always subordinate to the proclamation. The gospel message is proclaimed first and is followed with the proper teaching for those who respond to its message. Thus, even today, we ought first to get into the act of proclaiming, beseeching, appealing, and pleading with men to accept Jesus Christ as Lord and Saviour before we teach ethical applications.

The teaching message of the Bible is for those who have responded to Christ by accepting Him as Saviour and Lord. It is a message of how to respond to what God has done for us; it is a message of knowing the will of God and yielding to Him proper obedience. It gives ethical instruction for the life of the Christian; it spells out the meaning and the events of the life and death of Christ and how these apply to our lives here and now.

The teachings of the New Testament, however, do not cover every modern situation. The question of flying to the moon is not spoken to in the Bible. Does it mean then that the Bible has nothing to say on it? No, it does not. But what it does have to say will never be handed to us on a platter. The Word of God will remain a closed book until we take our search for the will of God seriously—until we stake our lives on it.

The tradition that the apostles received did not cover all the situations that man faces, not even in New Testament times.

How then did they meet such new circumstances? We can see from their own writings how they responded to new situations. We notice that the apostles were able to move out from the tradition that they had received into new situations. Under the guidance of the Holy Spirit they were able to interpret the meaning of the gospel to their contemporaries and to indicate its practical application in life even in new circumstances. In the same way, they were able to extend the meaning of what Christ had done to new areas.

Let us look at a few examples. The apostles had been shown by Jesus after the resurrection how the Old Testament prophecies pointed to His coming and how they were now fulfilled in Him. The Gospel writers in their writings continue this line of interpretation and, in Matthew and John particularly, we have account after account showing how prophecy was fulfilled. Such new insights were in harmony with the basic tradition (kerygma and didache) received. The Book of Hebrews spells out all kinds of new facets of what Christ has done by portraying Christ as the true High Priest. The Holy Spirit opened the eyes of the people to an ever-increasing understanding of the gospel message.

The Spirit of God also led the apostles to speak to ethical questions that had not been raised by Jesus but which seemed to follow logically from those which Jesus had presented. The way in which Paul no longer kept the laws of eating and drinking when with the Gentiles, nor required circumcision of Gentile Christians are illustrations. In all of this the gospel remained unaltered, but the ministry of the Holy Spirit enabled the Christians to better understand the gospel that they had received. It was alive with life.

In 1 Corinthians 7:10 Paul is asked some questions to which he can cite a word of the Lord (didache), but then he is asked a further question which he cannot answer this way. He, therefore, gives his own teaching (1 Cor. 7:25; 7:12) and simply indicates that he speaks as one who has the Spirit (1 Cor. 7:40b). There was, in other words, the activity of the Holy Spirit in their lives that not only helped them to recall the tradition, or the teaching of the Lord; but it helped them to spell out theologically and ethically the meaning of the gospel for their lives.

Does This Apply to Us?

We have all that the early Christians had. We have the tradition, the given, in that we have the Bible. We have both the kerygma and the didache. In addition to that, we have in the Bible an illustration of how the unchanging message was applied to new and different situations and contexts in life (e.g., the Gentile world). Above all, we have the Holy Spirit who will lead us in our attempts at applying the gospel in our own lives; He will lead us as we seek to apply the gospel to situations not encountered before in life.

It is not enough to know what the Bible has to say on a given question. We must also know something about the total circumstances (the context) in which a decision is to be made. The biblical command "you shall not steal" is perfectly clear in its meaning. But what does its application in your life mean? Is it stealing if I charge 300 percent profit on a manufactured article? You can see immediately that this depends on many other questions that have to be asked first. More than anything else it depends on our openness to the Spirit of God.

Let me illustrate. There is a whole range of meaning to the command "you shall not steal," depending on the extent to which we are open to the Spirit of God. 1) If I live in intimate fellowship with my Lord and Master, I do not steal because I would, in so doing, break the bond of fellowship with Christ. 2) To say that I do not steal because the Bible says it is a sin is to say something quite different. In this case, we are concerned more with an act than with a relationship. 3) When we say that we don't steal because of the teachings of the church and the family, or because of our conscience, then we have in mind a relationship to others and to ourselves; but it is already one step removed from the relationship that we have to Christ. 4) We can answer by saying we don't steal. We only take what is coming to us; or we don't steal for we have broken no laws. This is clearly a legalistic interpretation of stealing. It may follow the letter of the Word, interpreted according to a certain established code of what is or what is not stealing; but it opens the door to an unchristian ethic. It is then possible for our spirit to be totally selfish and covetous while yet abiding by an externally recognized code. 5) Finally, there may be such a lack of sensitivity to the Spirit of God that a Christian will hire a lawyer to find loopholes in the law in order that he may steal and yet not be legally charged with stealing.

It is evident from these illustrations that, even where the command is perfectly clear, we need the guidance of the Holy Spirit in applying this command to a specific life situation. We need to ask, therefore, How does the Spirit work in us to know God's will? Several conditions must be met by us before the Spirit of God will lead and direct us in *our* day.

1. We must be willing to obey. The Apostle Peter speaks of "having purified your souls by your obedience to the truth for a sincere love of the brethren" (1 Pet. 1:22). The Spirit of God leads us from truth to deeper truth only as we yield obedience to the knowledge and the insight that He has given us. Hans Denck stated that "no man can know Christ unless he follows after Him in life." It is not enough simply to read the words, the text, and expect to arrive at "truth." The New Birth is a prerequisite to the understanding of God's Word. So also is commitment to obedience in following the teachings of our Lord.

2. We must be growing Christians before we can receive the guidance of the Spirit in a particular situation. There is no standing still in the Christian faith. We either grow or become dwarfed in the faith. Read in this respect Hebrews 5:11-6:3. The writer indicates that we cannot gain spiritual insight at one time (let us say at the time of our conversion) and then retain it for the rest of life. If we do not continue to grow in the faith, we will lose what we once had and can no longer be trusted to know right from wrong (Heb. 5:13). That is, the one who does

not grow in the faith by continual obedience to the guidance of the Spirit loses his ethical sensitivity whether he has been a Christian many years or not.

3. To be spiritually sensitive, we must exercise our faith (Heb. 5:14). This means that we need to apply the faith anew to every situation in which we find ourselves. We must restudy what the Word of God means in our context of life, and we must restudy the context in life in the light of God's Word. It is not enough to simply apply a code of ethics that someone else has worked out. It must be our faith related to our lives.

4. There is always the danger that in applying the gospel we will tend to interpret it in the direction of our own carnal wants and desires. We tend so easily to confuse our own wishes and desires with the leading of the Spirit. To check this tendency we are admonished to exhort "one another" because of "the deceitfulness of sin" (Heb. 3:12, 13; 10:23-25). We need each other in the Christian faith. The will of God is not determined solely by our private interpretation of Scripture. The Spirit of God works through the Christian fellowship to stir us up to love and good works and to keep us from doing evil.

But after we have stated and fulfilled all of these pre-conditions, what then? How does the Spirit lead us to interpret rightly the Scriptures for our time? It is essentially a twofold process. It has to do with relating our understanding of the Word of God to our understanding of the present context of life. If we have a true understanding of both of these and a spirit of obedience to Christ, then we can trust the Spirit of God to lead us to know His will.

If we study the Scriptures in this way, we will exercise our faith and will grow in our understanding of the faith. We will grow in understanding the meaning of the gospel (doctrinal) and grow in the application of the gospel (ethics). To study the Scriptures in this way will cause God's Word to become alive to us in our own world.

But you say, this doesn't work. My friend and I (or our two

denominations) have the same Bible and the same Lord; we live in the same town and attend the same school; and, yet, we come away with different positions on almost every subject. Such a situation is very possible and it has already caused many unhappy divisions in the body of Christ.

Where such disagreement exists it is evident that we have homework to do. In such instances we have the obligation to wrestle together for the truth under the guidance of the Spirit. Usually we do not agree on either 1) what the Bible says, or 2) what the context or the situation in life is like.

In many instances we do not come with the same interpretation of the Scriptures. In such cases we must speak to the question of hermeneutics, i.e., the question of what principles to use in interpreting what the Bible says. This will be discussed in the following chapters.

For Further Study

Neil, William. *The Rediscovery of the Bible.* New York: Harper and Row, 1954.

Stibbs, Alan M. *Understanding God's Word.* London: IVF, 1950.

Chapter 8

Interpreting the Word

In the previous chapters we have dealt with some of the questions that must be settled before we can begin with interpretation. Too often we simply assume that these questions have been adequately dealt with and, therefore, do not give them a second thought. Similarly in interpretation, we tend to turn to commentaries on Scripture and, as a result, do not become familiar with the many disciplines or skills that contribute to the study of Scripture. It will be of help to us, therefore, simply to mention some of the basic disciplines that enter into the interpretation of Scripture.

Establishing the Canon

The first task is to determine which books should be considered as belonging to the Bible. This is necessary because the Christian church has sometimes included more books in the Bible than the present sixty-six books, and sometimes less. Some branches of the Syriac church do not include 2 Peter, 2 and 3 John, Jude, and Revelation. The Ethiopic Bible, on the other hand, includes two books that are not in our Bible today, Enoch and the Book of Jubilee. The Roman and the Greek Catholic Churches include the extra books which were included in the Septuagint (LXX), the Greek translation of the Old Testament. They, therefore, include in their Bible the books that are normally listed in the Apocrypha.

This is just to point out that there is not total agreement on which books belong to the Bible. The Protestant churches have by and large, however, always accepted the twenty-seven New Testament books and the thirty-nine Old Testament books which now make up the Bible.

Textual Criticism: Establishing the Text

None of the original manuscripts have survived. The oldest complete Hebrew Old Testament text is from the Medieval Period (A.D. 500-1500), and the oldest complete Greek New Testament manuscript still in existence is from the fourth century. We have individual manuscripts or fragments of manuscripts of the Old Testament going back to the first century B.C. and of the New Testament going back to about A.D. 135. Thus, as indicated earlier, we have only copies of copies. These copies at times give variant readings. It is, therefore, necessary to try to find which reading of the many variants in the thousands of manuscripts is the best reading. This discipline is known as textual criticism (lower criticism).

Before the text can be used for translation or interpretation, it must be established for its accuracy. We simply cannot do without this discipline. Very few people are competent or adequately trained for such work. But in the church there must always be those who will dedicate themselves to the work of textual criticism. In this way they help the rest of the church by determining the exact wording of the text to be used in the Bibles that are printed, and the text that is to be used in translating the Bible into other languages.

Great progress has been made in the understanding of biblical languages and in penetrating the thought patterns of the different nations, groups, and individuals. Similar progress has been made in understanding the changes that our own language has gone through. All this has made it necessary for Bible translations to be submitted to one revision after another.

Biblical Criticism

The various disciplines of criticism are necessary for us to learn something about the historical and literary context of the authors and the books we are to interpret. By *criticism* we mean nothing less than a careful examination of all the data and phenomena associated with the recording, preserving, and the interpreting of the Scriptures. Our use of the term should thus be a positive one. It should not be confused with a negative attitude to the Scriptures or any attempt to undermine God's Word.

Literary criticism has to do with a careful study of literary style, language, and vocabulary. This discipline has helped to draw appropriate conclusions concerning the unity, date of composition, origin, and authorship of the books of the Bible.

Literary criticism has brought a better understanding of the biblical and related languages and has lifted up the value of a careful literary study of the text of Scripture. It has also made its contribution in the knowledge of the grammar and vocabulary of the various biblical and related languages. There is not an exegetical commentary on the market today, whether conservative or liberal, that does not draw on the resources of the method of study known as literary criticism.

Historical criticism has to do with a careful study of the historical, cultural, and religious backgrounds of the writings of Scripture. If we are to understand the writings of an author, we will better be able to do so if we know something about the life and times in which he wrote. The biblical books, as we have indicated, originated at a specific time and place and under given circumstances. To know something of the conditions in which these books were written is to better understand the text itself. It does not guarantee a correct understanding of the text, but may help.

Historical criticism uses various tools and methods to describe history and background. It can use literary criticism mentioned above. It can also employ *archaeology,* the study of the material remains of man's past. Many of the things mentioned in the Scriptures can be corroborated in this way. It can be shown through archaeology that nomads invaded Egypt; that there was a flood similar to the one described in Genesis; and that the water conduit mentioned in 2 Kings 20:20 and the pool of Bethesda mentioned in John 5 actually existed. As long as archaeology is not used as a cheap apologetic to "prove" the Scriptures, it has a very valuable contribution to make to the study of the Bible.

Another way in which to cover background material has been to study the ideas and customs characteristic of the religious life of the neighboring nations. The danger in this type of study has been that scholars at times prematurely decided that the religion of Israel was nothing but a composite of all the types of religions they had encountered on their long journey from Mesopotamia to Egypt, to Canaan, to Babylon and in their contact with the nations of Persia, Greece, and Rome. This danger still exists, but again, if a study of the religion of the other nations is kept in proper focus, and the dissimilarities as well as the similarities noted, this discipline can make an excellent contribution to our study of the Scriptures. It provides a good background against which we can see the uniqueness of the events of revelation as we find them recorded in the Old and New Testaments.

Still another way in which we can get background material is simply to study *history*. Too often we have not really studied the history of Israel but rather isolated stories of David, Solomon, and the Prophets without regard to the actual historical events. When we look at the biblical accounts of history in the light of the knowledge about Israel and its neighbors that can be gained from other than biblical sources (archaeology: writings, clay tablets, etc.), then the biblical accounts receive a new realism. They become linked to the soil on which we walk and we receive a new appreciation for their humanness as well as for the way in which God participated in that history.

Form criticism is a discipline which seeks to study the life situation (*Sitz im Leben*) of the biblical writings. On the basis of the literary form of the writings it seeks to describe out of what context the biblical writings came. Thus, for example, the doxologies in various of Paul's letters may well have been formulations that were first coined in the worship service and later also used in the letters written to churches. The same could be said of songs and stories. Some of Paul's and Peter's instructions to women, slaves, and citizens are so similar that they can be shown to have originated in the ethical (paraenetic) instructions given to Christians.

Some radical scholars have used this discipline to call into question the teachings of Jesus, holding that the origin of the Gospels must be found in the early church; but again, apart from such radical scholarship the method of form criticism can help us to study the life of the church and the message of the gospel prior to its present literary form. In this way it is possible to say something about Israel or the early church, its confessions, its festivals, its worship, its oral teaching, and some of the literature of the Old and New Testaments.

None of these disciplines whether literary, historical, or form criticism can stand alone. They each in their own way help to furnish some, and only some, of the background knowledge that will be helpful to the interpreter in getting at the meaning of the text. It could even be said that we could do without such extra knowledge of the Bible, for the Bible itself furnishes enough of this information that we would not be helpless without it. Nevertheless, without it we would be a lot poorer in our understanding of the text, and many of the types of questions asked today require some background knowledge of this kind if we are to try to deal with them adequately.

Hermeneutics

We come now to some rules of the proper interpretation of the Scriptures. These rules are not the kind that, when applied in a mechanical way, will yield correct interpretation of Scripture. The interpretation of the Scriptures is not a mechanical process but an art—something that has to be carefully learned and practiced and for which some have a greater gift than others. A most helpful book in this area is *Protestant Biblical Interpretation,* by Bernard Ramm.

The following are some of the basic principles to be kept in mind when interpreting the Bible:

1. The language in which the text was written remains basic.

We should take care, first of all, to check the accuracy of our translations. The best way to do this is, of course, to learn the original languages. Where this is not possible, we can check on the accuracy of our translations by comparing them with other translations of the same or of another language. We can also use trustworthy authorities, for example, writers of commentaries to check on a particular translation.

2. Revelation, as has been stated, was given in history and man witnessed to this revelation in a specific period of time with a given language. We need to find out, therefore, what the people of the writer's own time would have understood him to say with the words and illustrations that he used. To know this will help us to understand how to interpret some of the expressions that were used to convey the author's thought. When we follow this procedure we will no longer be disturbed by such expressions as "bowels of mercy," for we will recognize that to the Greek this was thought to be the location of man's emotions.

3. We need to recognize that God revealed himself to Israel over a period of many centuries. It is, therefore, to be expected that man would be able to receive and understand more and more of God's revelation as time went on. Consequently, we have to be alert to observe a progression in man's understanding of God in the literature.

This does not mean that the early understanding of God is primitive and archaic. A fuller and more complete understanding of God was received by man until the time came when God could reveal himself in Christ Jesus our Lord.

4. There is also a principle to follow in terms of the Old and New Testaments. The Old Testament must be interpreted in the light of the fulfillment of the promise and of prophecy. It must be expounded in the light of Israel's history both before and after the revelation of Christ. In this way the Old Testament is understood in the light of the total revelation of God to Israel, out of whom He called the Messiah. Similarly, the New Testament must be interpreted in the light of God's revelation to Israel, to the people

of God in the first Covenant. Without this context of understanding much of the New Testament would have little meaning.

5. In interpreting a biblical book we must respect the time in which it was written. That is, we must interpret the book in its historical context. It would be wrong for instance, to assume that Genesis 1 answers directly to our nineteenth- and twentieth-century questions about evolutionary theories. These questions did not exist in that form in that day, and we cannot now assume that they were written to answer such questions.

6. We should always be careful to place checks on our own interpretations of the Scriptures. The first and most important check that we can apply is to check Scripture with Scripture. If there is lack of clarity, the passage that is clearest in meaning should be used to interpret the one that is less clear. In this way we will guard against making interpretations that clearly contradict Scripture.

We also need to check our interpretations against the great doctrinal formulations of the church, as for example, against the Apostolic Creed. This does not say that the interpretation is necessarily wrong if it does not agree verbatim with creeds, but it should say to us that we need to check and double-check where we come up with some interpretation that directly counters a formulation that has been affirmed by the church throughout the centuries.

Yet another check is to compare our findings with what others have written about the same passage or subject in commentaries, word studies, and Bible dictionaries. Such resource material is of great help as long as it does not become the main source of our interpretation. There is nothing that can substitute for a personal study of the Scriptures and for doing one's own preliminary study before resorting to sources of information.

Finally, we must also check our interpretation of the Scriptures against what we know of the world through other disciplines such as history, science, and anthropology. Care must be taken not to immediately reject our interpretation of the Bible the moment it does not correspond to the latest scientific theory. At times we may for many years simultaneously hold an interpretation of the Scriptures and an interpretation of the world that are contradictory to each other. We know that they cannot both be right. Either our interpretation of the Scriptures will turn out to be wrong or our interpretation of the world will be wrong or, in some instances, both will be wrong. We have the faith however, that what God has said through His creation of the world and through the revelation of His will in the Scripture, will not be contradictory, once both are fully understood.

In this way we recognize that science needs the perspective of faith in its own work; and the Bible interpreter needs the corrective of the scientist, so that he will not make assertions that are materially false. (Actually many scientific disciplines are used in the study of Scripture, e.g., archaeology.)

7. Another important principle to observe is that we should always be careful to read what the writer is trying to say. We should read out of the book (exegete) what the writer intended to say. Our temptation, however, is always that we will seek to read into the book (eisegete) what we want the author to say. This sounds self-evident as a principle of interpretation, but it is a difficult principle to follow in practice.

8. "No . . . scripture is a matter of one's own interpretation" (2 Pet. 1:20). The interpretation of a Scripture passage is not something that can be worked out individually, mechanically, or in separation from the Spirit of God and the community of faith. The Holy Spirit works not only through the individual but also through the community of believers, the church, to give us an understanding of God's will. We must, therefore, bring the interpretation of Scripture that we come to in our reading and study to the larger community of faith for its consideration and response. The church, through the work of the Holy Spirit, becomes a discerning community, or, as John Howard Yoder has termed it, the "hermeneutic community." It is not, in the last analysis, the specialized investigations or promulgations of the theologian that carry weight. They may help, but the Spirit of God can work

through any individual of the fellowship and through the entire fellowship of faith to lead us to know His will until we can repeat with the early church "it has seemed good to the Holy Spirit and to us. . ." (Acts 15:28).

9. We must be willing always to look at our own presuppositions that we bring to the interpretation of Scripture. This is where the greatest difficulties are encountered in interpretation. Because we approach the Bible with different presuppositions of faith, we do not come up with the same findings.

Every theology and every interpretation depends on a faith-principle from which the material and the discussion are viewed. Thus, for example, a liberal theologian has different faith-principles than a neoorthodox theologian or a fundamentalist theologian. If, for instance, an interpreter believes that miracles simply did not happen, then he must find some way to explain their presence in the Gospels other than that they are accurate factual reports. The most he could say is that they were reports of what people thought to have happened. Similarly, if a person believes that the Gospels as we have them today are the product of the early church, then he will have to find a totally different way of explaining their nature, origin, and composition than what we have used in lessons four and five.

Wherever we have such disagreements on the basic understanding of the gospel, we have homework to do. We should not react to it in terms of having no conversation with those who think differently. It should be to us a call to work harder and to seek fuller knowledge on the issue at hand. We must seek to come to a unity of spirit with all who confess that Jesus Christ is Lord.

In this lesson we have tried to speak to some of the principles of interpretation that should help us to draw closer together in our study of the Bible. May the Spirit of God lead us to know the truth as we yield our hearts in obedience to His Word.

For Further Study

Berkhof, Louis. *Principles of Biblical Interpretation.* Grand Rapids: Baker Book House, 1950.

Hofmann, J. C. K. von. *Interpreting the Bible.* Minneapolis: Augsburg Publishing House, 1959.

Mickelsen, A. B. *Interpreting the Bible.* Grand Rapids: Eerdmans, 1963.*

Ramm, Bernard. *Protestant Biblical Interpretation.* Natick: W. R. Wilde, rev. ed. 1956.*

Smart, James D. *The Interpretation of Scripture.* Philadelphia: Westminster Press, 1961.

---

*Recommended for the church library.

Chapter 9

From Text to Today

In the previous lesson we have been speaking about the large context of interpretation: the canon, the text, the background studies, and principles of interpretation. We now need to say something more specific about the application of such principles in our Bible study.

Exegesis

Exegesis is the application of the principles of interpretation to a specific unit of Scripture. The practical procedure of how to study a book will be outlined in the last chapter. What we want to do here is to look at the component parts of such a procedure without going into the details.

1. The first task of careful exegesis is to establish the text of the passage to be dealt with. The larger task of doing this for the whole Bible has already been referred to in a previous lesson and has been done for us by the textual critic. What remains to be done is to take note of and appraise the textual critic's findings. Variant readings of manuscripts upon which the text is based are frequently found in footnotes in our Bibles. For example, in Matthew 5:22 Jesus is quoted as saying "everyone who is angry with his brother shall be liable to judgment" (RSV). In the footnote it indicates that other ancient authorities insert *without cause*. It would then read "every one who is angry with his brother without cause shall be liable to judgment." There is quite a difference. The King James Version includes "without a cause." We need to confirm in our own mind whether the choice of the later critics is the right one.

2. Similarly, with respect to the text, the exegete has to de-

cide how it is to be translated. At times the same word can have two different meanings, depending on what we judge the writer to have intended. Thus, in 1 Peter 2:4 we have the choice of reading the opening words as a present participle ("to whom coming," KJV) or as an imperative ("come to him," RSV). We have even a clearer illustration of it in Hebrews 4:8 where the same name can mean either "Joshua" or "Jesus." The King James has used "Jesus" but the sense of the passage would call for Joshua's name to be read.

3. Besides determining the text and translating it, the exegete has to analyze the literary form of the passage in question. This step is essential if we are to know how the passage is to be approached. If it is historical narrative, then one approaches it as one would any historical account. If it is a parable, however, then one would immediately begin to look for the main point that the story wants to illustrate. If it is poetry, it is interpreted differently than biography.

4. With the help of the historical studies, referred to in the previous lesson, the exegete needs to determine the historical context of the passage. He needs to ask what is the life situation (*Sitz im Leben*) of the material he is interpreting. Some passages may be easily studied in this way, whereas, for others we simply do not have enough information to say very much about it. In many passages it makes a difference if we can say something about the historical text of a passage. If Paul says "Let everyone be subject to the governing authorities" (Rom. 13:1), the passage carries a new shade of meaning when we realize that Paul is here speaking against the influence of the Zealots who were trying to instigate revolt against Rome.

5. The passage, to be properly exegeted, has to be seen in its context in the book in which it stands. This will be spelled out in greater detail in the next lesson. The exegete must be aware of the immediate context of a passage. By *context* we mean what precedes and what follows the paragraph under discussion and how it is related to the purpose of the total book in which it stands.

6. Having done all this we can go on to determine the meaning of the text. We need first of all to know the meaning of the individual words used. How were they understood in the days of the writer? To get at the meaning of words we use the resources available to us in lexicons, dictionaries, word books, and concordances.

7. Once we know the meaning of the words we ask, what does the sentence say? This is determined largely from its grammatical and linguistic structure. The exegete must have a grasp of the language in which he works and be able to analyze sentences on the basis of the structure of the language. Finally, we ask, What is meant by the passage? What is the author seeking to say? In asking the question of the meaning of the text we are not yet asking for its meaning for us. We first ask what would the reader in his day have understood the writer to say. Once we have arrived at the answer to this statement, then we have exegeted the passage: we have given the meaning the author intended it to have in his day. This is, however, only the first thing that we want to understand. How do we move from the text to the present? Let us take one more step along this road.

Biblical Theology

When we have exegeted all the writings of a given author, we can go on to the next level of interpretation, that known as biblical theology. Simply stated, we want to get at all that the author believed and was seeking to communicate. Or in other words, we are seeking to get at the writer's theology (or the theology of all the biblical writers together).

Biblical theology is a rational (ordered) or a systematic study of the faith of the biblical writers. It seeks to understand the witness of the biblical writers as it was written and proclaimed in that day; it is an understanding of the proclamation seen from within, from the viewpoint of the writers themselves.

In biblical theology we seek to determine what they believed about God, about Jesus Christ, about God's revelation of himself, and about man's self-understanding. It speaks about the events that transpired in terms of how they were understood and interpreted by the eyewitnesses, that is, by the apostles.

We can arrive at a biblical theology in various ways. One way is to write down what an author emphasizes. If he devotes much space to one subject, it is obvious that this is central in his message. At times we can get at it by observing what words are repeated and become central or determinative in a particular author's writing. But whatever method we use, the task remains the same. We must get at the faith or belief of the writer himself.

Thus, for example, we notice in 1 Peter that the author always returns to the words "be subject." The citizens are to be subject to the emperor (2:13), the servants are to be subject to their masters (2:18), and women are to be subject to their unchristian husbands (3:1). Upon further examination, we notice that each one of the parties mentioned was being persecuted or mistreated because of his Christian faith. Each is exhorted to remain submissive in that difficult situation. This whole section, where Peter exhorts them to remain submissive, is followed with another main section in which the theme is suffering. It soon becomes clear that the author has a very strong theology of suffering. He is saying that the Christian is to stay where he is even though he is being persecuted. We can then see what Peter believed. It was his belief that the suffering of the Christian will in the end be the best witness that he can give of his faith to the non-Christian world. This is what he believed on the basis of what Christ had done (1 Peter 2:20ff.). The next section will deal with the question of whether we should give the same counsel to the church in the twentieth century.

Once the theology of the individual writers has been worked out, we can compare them with each other and thus arrive at the composite picture which we know as biblical theology.

Still another way in which we can get at biblical theology is to follow one basic theme through the Old and New Testaments. In this procedure care must be taken not to take passages out of their context and use them merely as proof texts of a theme that we ourselves have in mind. In using this particular method it is helpful to use a rather broad or basic theme in order to avoid this danger.

This is the difficulty which former doctrinal studies often ran into when they simply chose a theme and then listed all the Scripture passages which might apply to it. It did not sufficiently take into consideration the historical context of the writing or the author's understanding or interpretation of the gospel.

Systematic Theology

In systematic theology we apply the fruit of biblical exegesis and biblical theology as we seek to understand what the Bible is saying to us today.

Systematic theology is a systematic study of what it means to accept the biblical faith in our day. It seeks rationally to understand the faith in terms of the knowledge that we have both of the Bible and of the world today. Thus, for example, if we speak of conversion today we speak of it in such a way that it will not violate our own self-understanding—an understanding given to us, at least in part, by such disciplines as sociology and psychology. Systematic theology speaks, in other words, of the events of Christ's life, death, and resurrection in terms of our present understanding of the Word and the world.

We are not greatly helped by studying systematic theology of a century ago, other than that it is always helpful to know the history of a particular discipline. Often it is not helpful simply because in another period of time different questions were being asked, questions that are no longer being asked. The questions we bring to the faith today have moved to new areas because we are confronted with different temptations and challenges. For example, we do not particularly concern ourselves any longer with the question of when the soul is born in the fetus, but it used to be a very important question.

Systematic theology by its very nature is modern in the sense of being up-to-date. It speaks to the latest questions and addresses itself to these questions in the full awareness of the fact that the gospel as such has not changed. The gospel remains, but it is now being applied or related to new problems—the problems that modern man has not yet sufficiently answered for himself. Once the question has been spoken to in sufficient detail and with sufficient clarity and has become available to all in the form of books or public discussion, then we may turn away from these questions to deal with new questions that have not yet been clarified.

We need to see, therefore, that it is much more the biblical theology that remains unchanged and unchanging rather than systematic theology. This is as it should be. Biblical theology does not change except as perhaps a wrong understanding of it is corrected in a later period of time. On the other hand, our own understanding of what the gospel means for us and for all mankind is a growing one. We today have the benefit of many centuries of work in which able men have expounded for us the meaning of the gospel. Man does not stand still in his appreciation and interpretation of the gospel. This growth and development of understanding is reflected in systematic theology. Systematic theology must always be dynamic in the sense of growing in its depth and breadth.

In studying the history of systematic theology, we become aware of the fact that in each period of history the church has sought to solve a particular problem or doctrine. This is so, not only for an individual denomination, but for the church as a whole. At first it was the establishing of the canon, next the understanding of the two natures of Christ, then the teachings on the Trinity, and more recently the question of Scripture being the sole authority for faith and practice. Today we are working on a new set of questions which have to do with the interpretation of Scripture; the relation of "sacred" and "secular"; and whether or in what way God is at work outside of the church. These are not easy problems and it may take many years to work through them just as it took years to work through the problems that the early church and the church of the Middle Ages and the Reformation faced.

We return now to the question of how the Bible speaks to us today. In lesson 7 we mentioned that there were two components involved in the Bible speaking to us: 1) our understanding of the message of the Bible, and 2) our understanding of the world or the human situation to which the Word is to be applied. In the last two chapters we have been speaking largely about how to know what the Bible says. This is the most important, for we need to know what God's Word is all about before we can apply it to life. But we must now also give some attention to the problem of understanding the context in which our decisions are made.

Let us state negatively, first of all, that we should not jump into the twentieth century with every Bible verse. Because Peter advised women not to braid their hair (1 Pet. 3:1-6) does not mean that we so advise women not to braid their hair. What we must do in such cases is to get at the basic principle the author applied to the problem in his day. It is obvious that he did not want Christians to conform to the world or to give the impression that they were something that they were not, i.e., unchaste or irreverent. If we then apply this principle in our day we may get many different admonitions which all would be true to this verse. Think of some illustration.

In the above illustration, we see how there has to be an evaluation or an understanding of the present human context before a right application of Scripture can be made. But let us take a more difficult example.

Under biblical theology above, we mentioned that the Apostle Peter had a well-developed theology of suffering and witness. It was his understanding that the servant should remain with a crooked master (1 Pet. 2:18) and a Christian wife was to remain with her non-Christian husband even if this would mean suffering. In such suffering they would give a witness to the faith. In fact Peter says "to this you have been called" (1 Pet. 2:21).

How can we now bring this into the twentieth century? Does it mean we go back to slavery? Does it mean we sit back and let

98

ourselves be clobbered by one and all? Hardly! Again, we have to get at the basic principle that Peter applies. As far as I can see, the principle is that exactly where our Christian faith cuts across man's sin, and we are called upon to suffer for it, we give the clearest testimony to our faith. This is what Christ did in allowing even His life to be taken by man in his sin.

Such a principle is not easy to apply. It means that in every situation we must be prepared to suffer for being Christian; it is a call to be Christian in our vocations and be willing to suffer for it. Thus a doctor must be Christian first and then follow medical ethics and practice only as far as he can. A businessman must in all things be Christian regardless whether he can compete with the world or not (he may have to suffer for it). A laborer must be Christian first, etc. The principle that Peter applies might be more familiar to us if we did not let our vocational ethics come first and Christian ethics second.

This illustration gives us the opportunity of seeing two possible approaches that should be avoided. It would be possible for us to look at 1 Peter 2:11—3:7 and conclude that Christians should maintain the status quo. Or, what is worse, use it to show that the New Testament has nothing to say about social reform. It is clear that Peter does not maintain the status quo. He is suggesting the changing of men, and therefore society, by bringing into it a new way of dealing with evil—Christian suffering. It is accomplished simply by the Christian actually being Christian in that society.

The second approach that must be avoided is the opposite extreme. The above error emphasizes the biblical text without reference to the human situation. If we take the opposite extreme, we may make decisions by looking only at the human situation and by completely ignoring the biblical teaching. We would then decide that the passage speaks to a situation that is not present today and, therefore, has no contribution to make except maybe of a sentimental or devotional nature.

Let us take another problem of interpretation: Genesis chapter 1 and science. The task of systematic theology is after all to spell out how the faith is related to our knowledge of the world gained through other disciplines. Let us note the following without going into great detail.

Upon careful reading it appears evident that Genesis 1 is a poetic rather than a scientific description. It, therefore, cannot be used as a scientific textbook and it will not answer the scientific questions we bring to it.

We are, however, rational creatures and feel the compulsion to harmonize Genesis 1 with our present knowledge of the world (geology and biology etc.). Any such harmonization, however, is created by man's present reasoning and should never be confused with the message of Scripture.

Many different theories have been invented to bridge the gap between Scripture and science. The Concordist view sought to find exact parallels between science and the Bible but with the danger of doing violence to both science and the Bible; both are made to fit *our* particular view. Others have tried to argue that God first created a "good" world which later *became* "without form and void" (Gen. 1:2). God then refashioned the world and this accounts for the differences in what science finds and Scripture reports. It uses two worlds to explain the difficulties, but this too is problematic.

Even if one takes only writers who profess to accept the verbal plenary view of inspiration, one has a great variety of positions taken on how science relates to Scripture. Thus, for example, Harry Rimmer (*Modern Science and the Genesis Record*) insists that a "day" in Genesis 1 has to be viewed as twenty-four hours. This is a literal reading of Scripture but next to impossible to correlate with science. E. J. Carnell (*An Introduction to Christian Apologetics*) speaks of a "threshold evolution" in which he sees a wide range of change within the "kinds" originally created of God. This view is less literal but correlates better with the findings of science. Bernard Ramm (*The Christian View of Science and Scripture*) holds to "progressive creation." The "day" must be interpreted as symbolic ("with the Lord one day is as a thousand years," 2 Pet. 3:8). Progress and development in the world are seen as the continued activity of God the Creator. H. N. Ridderbos (*Is There a Conflict Between Genesis 1 and Natural Science?*) tries to be true to the fact that Genesis 1 is poetic literature. He finds here a schematic presentation of six days. There are two sets of three days each, in which there are eight creative acts introduced by the words "and God said." The two sets of three days complement each other. In this way "day" could mean twenty-four hours for that matter, but it is a poetic and not a scientific description.

Thus we can readily see that each man makes his own harmonization. But these are all tentative suggestions at best. They may help us in our rational understanding of the faith, but they remain *our* conclusions based on *our* knowledge of the world and of Scripture and are arrived at through *our* reasoning.

If we want to know what Genesis 1 has to say, we must look to what the writer intends to say in and to his generation (see pp. 19, 20). The central assertion is that God made all that constitutes this universe in which we live.

We return to what we have said earlier. The proper application of the Scriptures requires that 1) we diligently search for a clear understanding of what the Bible says; 2) that we inform ourselves as completely as possible on the human situation in which we must act; and 3) that we be open to the guidance of the Holy Spirit and willing to yield obedience to the knowledge of the truth received.

These last two lessons may have tended to say to some that we have made it much too complicated. Not really. What we have tried to do is simply to put in words what we actually do all the time when we study the Scriptures. What this should do is help us to become more conscious of the process of study so that we can more easily correct ourselves when our study is not fruitful. Now move on to the next lesson with paper, pencil, and Bible in hand. Soon you will find that once you start studying the Bible on your own, what we have considered here will take on new meaning.

Chapter 10

Some Guidelines for Bible Study

Much of what has been said in the previous lessons will have relatively little meaning unless we actually study the Bible. It is not enough to study *about* the Bible. What we have considered thus far is to be a help in Bible study itself. We have considered the general setting for further Bible study and a general framework within which to place what we study in various sections of the Bible. But now let us consider how we actually might study a portion of Scripture.

The Difference Between Bible Study and Bible Reading

Bible study is carried on in many and various ways. The usual procedure is to read a chapter a day, beginning with Genesis or with Matthew. Some read one chapter in the Old Testament and one in the New Testament each day. Others open their Bibles only occasionally, once a week or several times a month, and read longer portions.

Such reading is usually done in a meditative mood with the hope that some phrase or verse or section will provide food for spiritual nourishment. The person who reads his Bible in this way entertains the hope that the Lord will send a word of encouragement for his situation here and now.

What has been described above is not really Bible study in the best sense of that word. Rather, this is devotional reading.

Bible study is more intense. When a person studies the Bible he assumes the stance of a student. He approaches his work systematically. He engages in research. He uses tools to accomplish his task. Bible study is an art that needs to be practiced and learned.

Principles to Guide the Christian in Bible Study

So that we might better understand how to study the Bible, let us set down some guidelines:

1. The amount of biblical content which the person covers in Bible study is not of particular importance. We cannot assume that the Christian who has read his Bible from cover to cover is necessarily a good Bible student. He may not have studied the Bible at all. Some students of the Bible have spent as much time studying one single word in the Scriptures as it would take another person to read the whole Bible. The first person may have been doing thorough Bible study and the second person not. The point is this: Bible study depends on whether the student has understood, not upon whether he has read many chapters.

2. The Bible student should first seek to understand the passage or the chapter or the book for what it said to *its time* before he draws applications for the present day. This is a rule of thumb and not an absolute statement. Christians have been led by the Spirit to see the relevance of a passage of Scripture for their situation in an instance. This is less common, however, and probably the more precarious way of interpreting Scripture. It is better to ask first what the message of the prophet of Isaiah meant for the people of the eighth century before one asks what it means for today.

The first step in Bible study is to understand the passage which one is reading; to be able to say it in one's own words; and to know what it meant for those who first heard it or read it.

It is our tendency to read a twentieth-century interpretation into the Bible text. This is a subtle sin. Rather, we should be reading a biblical interpretation into the twentieth-century situation. This would give us light.

3. The phrase or sentence or verse or paragraph or chapter which one is studying should always be considered in the light of

the larger context in which one finds the passage. For example, when one studies Ephesians 3:1-6 one should keep the message of the entire chapter in mind, and one should take the message of the entire letter to the Ephesians into consideration. The large context will shed light upon one's understanding of the smaller passage, and the smaller passage will shed light upon one's understanding of the letter as a whole. It works both ways.

Most Christians know Isaiah 1:18 from memory: "Come now, let us reason together, says the LORD: though your sins are like scarlet. . . ." But have you ever read the entire first chapter of Isaiah to understand why this was said in the first place, to find out what the sins of the people were, and to discover how their sins could be forgiven?

A Method of Studying the Bible

There are many methods of Bible study. No one method is the best. However, some have been proved to be more helpful than others and to get at the heart of the passage better than others. Here is one method of Bible study that may be of help to you.

Begin by choosing a passage of Scripture for study. This may be an entire chapter or a shorter portion such as a paragraph. Most of the New Testament lends itself to logical divisions for study: a parable or a series of parables, or a miracle or series of miracles, or a series of sayings by our Lord.

Ask six questions of the passage you have chosen: who, where, when, how, what, and why. With pencil and notepaper in hand, begin to make notes on your observations.

1. *Who* are the persons or groups of persons in the passage? Make a list of them as you read. Group them, placing individuals in one group and groups of persons (for example, Israelites, Pharisees, Corinthians) in another. Group them again, placing the primary characters (the main persons and groups of persons) in one list and the secondary characters (those in the background of the passage) in another.

Make certain you understand who these persons are. If the

words *sinners* and *tax collectors* appear on your list, it may help to take a Bible dictionary and read the articles concerning these groups so you understand exactly who they were. Do not assume that you can read a twentieth-century interpretation into these terms. If the references to persons are vague, for example, "a whole people" (Amos 1:6), you may want to take a Bible commentary to check on the meaning of such references.

Now all of this may take as much time as you normally allot for one Bible study sitting. This is as far as one may get in an hour's Bible study at church. But that is no cause for uneasiness. The study can be continued. By the time the student has listed all persons in the passage, he has read the passage thoroughly two or three times with a purpose. And best of all, he has been forced to concentrate on the living dynamic, the persons and relationships between persons, which makes the passage live in the first place. He has begun to consider the event behind the account.

For some passages of Scripture, the study of persons involved in the account is quite far-reaching. Take Luke 15 for example. Here we have the original situation where tax collectors and sinners draw near to hear Jesus. Some Pharisees and scribes object and Jesus tells three parables. The first one is about the shepherd and his hundred sheep. Secondary figures in this parable are the shepherd's friends and neighbors (Lk. 15:6), a sinner who repents, and ninety-nine just persons (Lk. 15:7). The second is about a woman who loses a coin. Secondary figures are the friends and neighbors (Lk. 15:9) and the one sinner (Lk. 15:10). The third is about a man and his two sons. Secondary figures are the citizen of a far country (Lk. 15:15), the father's hired servant (Lk. 15:17f.), and the elder son's friends (Lk. 15:29).

In addition, other persons must be taken into account as well. The writer of the Gospel is Luke and he writes to Theophilus on the basis of what has been told to him by eyewitnesses and ministers. One does not fully understand the parables if one does not take into account that Luke is addressing a Gentile (a lost sheep and coin and son), a representative of the non-Abrahamic people like the tax collectors and sinners with whom Jesus is now associating.

These observations about persons are essential for a right interpretation of the passage.

2. *Where* did the event take place? For the most part this involves Bible geography, and in some cases more specifically the question of location, for example, within a city temple. For some passages the geographical question is easily settled. In general, it is not too difficult to determine where the passion narrative has its setting, although even the knowledgeable Bible reader needs to review specific places within Jerusalem now and then. For other passages it is difficult to determine the setting. Sometimes we simply venture a guess. Up-to-date commentaries are dealing more seriously with the question of location and offer much help.

In any case, it is important to know where the event recorded in the passage has its setting. Some of the comments made by Jesus, and recorded in the Gospels, gain specific meaning when one knows that they were said in the context of His Galilean ministry and not during His Judean ministry. Amos' message must be understood in the light of the situation in northern Israel and in view of the fact that a prophet from southern Israel was speaking the Word of God to the northern sector.

Let us consider Luke 15 once again. The question *where* has several parts to it. a) Where were the parables first spoken by Jesus? b) Where did Luke record his Gospel? c) What larger geographical area did Jesus have in mind when He thought of the application of the teaching of the parables?

By now the Bible student has read his passage at least twice and possibly five or six times. He has begun to think into the living event behind the written account in terms of the persons involved and the places where the event(s) occurred.

3. *When* did the events happen? This is the question of date. Again the student cannot always determine the answer. And it matters more with some passages than with others. When the passage relates to Old Testament history, the question of date

must not be overlooked. When the passage is from the Gospels, it matters at what stage in the ministry of our Lord the event occurred. When one studies Ephesians there should be some consciousness of the place of the Ephesian letter in the ministry of the Apostle Paul. At first this may not seem to make much difference; but, as the Christian becomes more conversant in the Scriptures, he will make use of this information in biblical interpretation.

For Luke 15 the question of date has several aspects: a) When did Jesus speak these parables? When did this clash between himself and the self-righteous Pharisees and scribes happen? Was it late in His ministry or early? And a further question is, Were these parables originally all spoken at one occasion, or did Luke gather them and place them here in this order? Sometimes one can get a lead on the latter question by comparing similar accounts in the other Gospels. In the case of Luke 15, this does not help because these parables are not found in Matthew, Mark, or John. b) When were these parables written down by the Gospel writer? Or were they perhaps written down somewhere else by someone else first? Take note of the spread of years between the time Jesus would have told them early in the first century and the time they were written by Luke later in the first century. Use your imagination to visualize in what kinds of ways these parables may have been used before they were recorded by Luke. c) And finally, when does Jesus expect the parables to be applied?

By now we are already tempted to make preliminary observations. We see that our Lord has the entire scope of history in mind from creation to the present. At first all were in the shepherd's flock and in the widow's hand and in the father's house. But then some became lost: the Gentiles, the tax collectors and sinners, Theophilus, we. But the Creator is concerned that these who have wandered away know the door is open. They may return and be fully reinstated as sons. Of course, those who were always at home, the Abrahamic people, the Pharisees and scribes, the self-righteous ones, will not like it. But the Father wills it. And this is what Jesus is trying to demonstrate (Lk. 15:1,2).

4. *How* is the passage stated? This is the question of mood and style. It is important to recapture the mood of the passage. This is not an easy task because we have the written word but cannot hear the spoken word. The mood is easily caught when one hears the words being spoken but not so easily when one only sees them written.

For example, a father can say "It's bedtime" to his son in different moods. If this is the kind of matter-of-fact announcement the father makes at nine o'clock every evening, an announcement to which the son always responds at once, then the mood will likely be mild. But if the son is not in the habit of listening to these words, and if we are hearing the father say "It's bedtime" for the third time within ten minutes, the mood will be more intense, perhaps even angry. So the mood depends to some extent upon the situation and upon the response expected by the speaker from his hearers.

The mood also depends upon the personality of the person proclaiming the announcement. Perhaps we know the father as one who does not raise his voice and whose very precise way of speaking does not require an angry outburst. We then assume something about the way he will speak to his son under any situation. The mood depends to some extent upon the personality of the speaker.

Read one of the psalms. What is the overall mood? Joy? Praise? Thanksgiving? Repentance? Wrath? Anger? And as you examine the psalm more closely you may find the mood changing from repentance at the beginning to praise toward the end. The mood of the psalm will influence one's interpretation.

What observations can we make about the mood of the Luke 15 incident? The situation begins when some outcasts draw near to hear Jesus. They are interested in what He is saying, for seemingly this a word of hope for them. But then the Pharisees and scribes come with their objections and murmurings, and an argumentative mood sets in. In the midst of this tension where the whole tradition of a community is being called into question on the one hand and some castaways hear a comforting word on the other hand, Jesus speaks the three parables. We sense the mood.

Further, there is the question of style. Here we ask, for example, whether the passage under consideration should be taken literally or figuratively, as for example, some of the passages in Ezekiel or in Revelation. We also study similes and metaphors to try to understand why they are used and what they mean.

The student must also take the overall literary style into account. Remember that the history sections of the Old Testament are chronicles for the most part, that the Psalms are hymns and congregational responses, that the prophetic writings were probably first spoken in short sermon-like sayings in public, and that Paul's writings are letters. Try to get away from looking at the passage as so many words objectively brought together. Try to relive the original situation as you consider the text.

5. *What* is said? In the approach outlined here we have not neglected the content of the passage thus far. In order to find out who the persons are, where and when the event occurred, and how it was stated, we could not overlook content. But now we are ready to consider what is said in detail.

The usual way to do Bible study is to start with the question of what is said. We have pushed it back purposely, so that we come to the content with some sensitivity to the living situation into which the content was written or spoken or acted. The Bible student should be ready by now to make some fairly accurate and meaningful observations about the content of the passage.

At this point it might be helpful to draw a horizontal line, marking the verses on the line as in the illustration below. Heavier vertical lines can indicate new paragraphs and larger divisions. For Luke 15, the outline may look something like this:

Luke 15   Three Parables About the Lost

1 - 2	3 - 7	8 - 10	11 - 24 25 - 32
Introduction	The Lost Sheep	The Lost Coin	The Lost Son

One might now write a descriptive sentence under each paragraph title. This sentence sums up the thought of the paragraph. The student may choose to work in even greater detail and write a sentence to describe each step in the sentence of the passage. Leave room for later additions.

As the student tries to sum up the content of the passage, he practices the art of forgetting all former impressions he might have had about the passage. He approaches it as though this were his first encounter with the material. In this way he allows for the possibility of making new and fresh observations. There is the good possibility that for years and years one has had erroneous impressions of what certain biblical passages are talking about.

Some satisfaction should come to the student when he can sit back and say: This passage of Scripture can be summed up as follows.

6. *Why* does the passage occur in the Scriptures? This question has a double focus. First, what purpose did the passage serve for its time—for Bible times? And secondly, what purpose does it serve for our times?

The answer to the first question should have become at least somewhat clear to us by now, but needs to be thought of specificially in any case. The answer to the second question is not so easy to come by. In fact, this has been the great problem for Christians in all times. How is the Word of God brought to bear upon the present generation?

Does the person who stands in the pulpit on Sunday mornings have the final say about applying the Scriptures to our times? Does each individual Christian follow the inclinations of his own heart and apply the Word as he sees fit? Does there need to be consensus in the company of believers before one can take an application of the Word as valid? These are just three simple possibiilties, and each has both limitations and commendations. The large question is the one about the working of the Holy Spirit. He is not limited to any one channel. But when do we know that He has been working in us and among us?

The problem we find ourselves in when we want to apply the Word in our day is a healthy one, because if we are serious about doing so, we will find ourselves being driven back to the Bible again and again to check our application of the Word. And so the Christian moves from Bible study to Christian living and back again to Bible study, only to repeat the cycle. In this tension, and by the grace of God which covers our humanness, we continue our pilgrimage in this world.

Why was Luke 15 preserved for us? The answer has several facets. a) Jesus was saying something highly important for the Jewish-Gentile community in His day. He was pleading with the self-righteous religious Jews, asking them to open their arms to the Gentile community. His argument was that God is Father of all men, and He is even now inviting the Gentile community into His grace. Jesus illustrates this himself by speaking with the tax collectors and sinners. b) Luke 15 is for us in the sense that we are non-Jews. We are tax collectors and sinners. We are Gentiles. Jesus came for us. c) The application reaches beyond this categorization of the human race, however. Jesus was against exclusion, against self-righteous possession of the goodness of the Creator God. The passage cautions us that we could also fit the shoes of the Pharisees and scribes, thinking that the Christ is only for us. Instead He is for all people, the religious and the not-so-religious.

Tools for Bible Study

In the course of our study we will use tools to help us in research. For the *who* question nothing will help as much as a good Bible dictionary. The *New Bible Dictionary* edited by J. D. Douglas is one example of an up-to-date resource book.

For the *where* question a good atlas will help. *The Westminster Historical Atlas to the Bible* is especially good. Not all "where" questions can be answered with an atlas. For some a Bible commentary will need to be consulted.

There is no one source book which gives the key to the *when* question. For Old Testament history some recent histories of Israel are available. John Bright's *A History of Israel* or F. F. Bruce's *Israel and the Nations* could be considered.

The mood and style of the passage can be sensed best in the actual reading of the text. Commentaries shed light on this aspect of Bible study.

What is said in the passage is learned most accurately by a careful reading of the text. Commentaries should be used where meanings are unclear.

The *why* question is, for the most part, to be dealt with through observation. There are probably no better tools for finding ways of applying the Bible to our present day than a keen sensitivity to the concerns and issues abroad in our contemporary world.

*   *   *   *   *

ABOUT THE AUTHOR

David Schroeder teaches Bible, ethics, and philosophy at the Canadian Mennonite Bible College, Winnipeg, Manitoba. He is a native of the province of Manitoba. He received the B.Th. degree from Mennonite Brethren Bible College, Winnipeg; A.B. from Bethel College, North Newton, Kansas; B.D. degree from Mennonite Biblical Seminary, Chicago; and earned a Doctor of Theology degree at the University of Hamburg, Germany. He has also studied at Garrett Biblical Institute, Chicago, and Goshen College, Goshen, Indiana.

He has served as a pastor in Winnipeg for several years and is active as a leader of ministers' conferences and Bible conferences in Canada and the United States.